Dancing on a Crack
IN A HOLLOW HOUSE

Dancing on a Crack
IN A HOLLOW HOUSE

MY BROKEN STORY
THROUGH *Harm* TO *Hope*

Kathryn Traub

Love You, Vicki

Kathy

2023

Charleston, SC
www.PalmettoPublishing.com

Dancing on a Crack in a Hollow House

First Edition

Hardcover ISBN: 979-8-8229-0772-0
Paperback ISBN: 979-8-8229-0773-7

For Janice and Christine,
One day we will hold hands and dance together
through Heaven's fields of glorious fragrant flowers
where every tear is wiped away, and there will be no more
death, sorrow, or crying. Neither shall there be any more pain,
for the former things will have passed away.

Contents

Foreword

I am both honored and humbled to write the foreword for Kathy's memoir. I am also terrified that I won't be able to do justice to her remarkable message.

I met Kathy Traub in 1985, when her twelve-year-old daughter auditioned for a musical I was directing for the local community theater. I cast her very talented daughter, Heather, and thus began our long, beautiful friendship. It was almost an immediate connection. The most accurate way to describe Kathy is to say "open-hearted."

When Kathy slowly unfolded her tragic childhood to me, I felt like she walked out of a horrifying past, and I wondered how such a beautiful soul could have survived and grown from such a background. Her experience was so foreign to me. Yes, I was aware that such tragedies existed but not where they intersected my world. I guess one could say that Kathy took the scales off my eyes. I suddenly became aware and then, as if a curtain were lifted, I began hearing of this insidious evil rearing its head in other friends' families and, eventually, within my own family.

According to the CDC,

- about one in four girls and one in thirteen boys in the United States experience child sexual abuse;
- someone known and trusted by the child or child's family members perpetrates 91 percent of child sexual abuse.

Because there are so many unreported cases, most probably these numbers are greatly underestimated.

There is an ocean of wounded victims, survivors, who need this kind of book to find hope and healing, but even more it's for people, like I was, who are oblivious of this rampant attack on our country's children. The scales need to be removed from our eyes. We need to be vigilant for those who need our help, our encouragement, our protection.

Angie Ellis
Associate Professor OSU
English High School Teacher
MA Theater

Preface

For years I have felt a strong prompting to write my story. It wasn't until I retired in 2021, and a worldwide pandemic and lockdown struck, that I diligently began the arduous task of finishing putting my story to words.

I believe that endeavoring to understand our own unique stories and how they have shaped us is essential to our well-being. We are each the product of the stories we have lived, the stories we have heard, and even the stories we have never been told. The colorful threads woven into the tapestry of our stories, whether they are healthy, broken, or frayed, shape us, providing the lens of how we see ourselves, the world, and our place in it.

In addition, examining our story allows us to determine how our future chapters evolve. We can move from a bystander to an active participant, directing the here and now and what is to come. Yes! New chapters can be written, breaking the harmful cycles of so many broken stories.

In this book, my story does not unfold in chronological order. Rather it is told in intermixed timelines, sometimes expressed in the third person, and sometimes expressed in my own voice, to illustrate snippets of my life and glimpses of the people and events that all have shaped my story.

Finally, I believe sharing our stories connects us and has the potential to help someone else feel they are not alone. This is my hope, that by sharing portions of my story, I might shine light on the darkness of abuse and encourage others to find their voice and strength to coauthor beautiful new chapters in their own lives.

Warmest Regards,
Kathy

CHAPTER 1

The Indelible Mark

I let out a shudder as the nippy air leaves goosebumps along my skin. Did I turn down the air last night? I step across the kitchen and prepare a pot of coffee to warm me up. Just as the coffee begins to brew, I check the thermostat and adjust the temperature to seventy degrees. Undeniably an invigorating new chill is in the air. Just outside the kitchen window, leaves adorned in their splendid farewell attire of rustic hues flutter gracefully through a soft breeze before relinquishing their last ounce of life and falling to the ground.

It is a beautiful, crisp fall morning. From a distance, the echoing sound of the Coho ferry horn nourishes my spirit. Like the comfort of a familiar voice, the sounding of this unique morning ritual is becoming my newest friend.

I make my way to the living room window for one last glimpse of Travis and Heather. Pressing close against the glass, I closely watch them as a warm shaft of light from the early morning sun embraces my face. My eyes are glued to them and an affectionate smile spreads across my lips as their beloved picture-perfect frames travel down the sidewalk toward their new school. Of course, it doesn't surprise me, Heather is a foot or two ahead of Travis and seems intent on being on time, while he seems more interested in kicking his way through a pile of damp leaves. I strain for the very last glimpse of them, but they inevitably vanish from my sight. Watching them venture away stirs a host of emotions. Everything in our world is new—a new school, a new home, and a new family. Silently I ask God to take care of them.

I grab the empty box of Honey Nut Cheerios they polished off and scoop up their cereal bowls from the kitchen table. *How many times must I remind them to take their dirty dishes to the sink?* I quibble to myself, just as a loud commotion bellows from the family room, redirecting my attention. Blaring from the RCA console TV, the silly "crime-solving" dog, Scooby Doo, and his buddy Shaggy are in a hot pursuit, radiating a ton of ruckus. Eager to end the noisy disturbance, I reach for the off button. Relieved, I take a deep breath as near quiet descends on the house. Finally, the early-morning hustle and bustle have ceased.

I meander from room to room, making beds and placing treasured stuffed animals carefully upon pillows. Every knick-knack is situated perfectly. Heather, now seven years old, has books scattered on her bedroom floor. I discover one of her favorites, *Little House on the Prairie*, buried under the covers. I retrieve the hidden book and reason to myself, *She is just like her grandma, with her nose always buried in a book. Even when we are on vacation, we can't pry her away from the novel she is lost in!* Still, without a doubt, I am grateful she inherited this wonderful trait. Carefully I collect and stack each book on her nightstand so each title can easily be read.

In Travis's room, on hands and knees, I watchfully run my fingers through the carpet, gathering up a multitude of LEGO pieces. Scooping up each tiny piece, I grin, ever so thankful these are the ones I won't step on or suck up with the vacuum.

While I place them in containers ready for his next creative endeavor, my mind wanders into the future, and I imagine him as a budding engineer or architect.

I move down the hallway, where a gallery of family pictures hangs. Gently I dust the tops and edges of each treasured photo. The numerous photos tell a story. I take a moment, cherishing the baby pictures of Travis and Heather, astonished at how fast the years are flying by and how much they have grown and changed. My eyes move to our recent wedding photo. For a moment the intimate photograph catches my breath. This candid photo, taken of us just after saying our vows, captures perfectly a mixture of our joy and butterflies. As I continue down the gallery, there is no question that Bill, an only child, was adored. In one photo Bill is bursting with pride in his Eagle Scout uniform, while another shows him in his climbing gear in the Olympic Mountains. In another picture he is handsomely donning his navy service dress. Seventeen years my senior, my husband has years of important history displayed in this priceless gallery. Finished, I stand back and take one last look at the treasured keepsakes, ensuring not one frame is out of line.

This ceremonial act of ensuring order brings me some semblance of well-being and security. After all, we have only been in this house for a couple of weeks. Oh, how I anticipate the day it will completely feel like home. At last, with the house picked up and tidy, I settle contentedly into the soft living room sofa. The warmth of the glistening sun now fills the room. Relaxing in this moment of quiet, myriad thoughts somersault through my mind and are married with hope and expectancy. I think to myself, *This is our new beginning, our special moment.* My heart is full of promise, and I'm certain nothing can spoil this beautiful day.

Quietly nestled between the Strait of Juan de Fuca and the Olympic Mountains, our new home, Port Angeles, Washington, is a town populated with as many taverns as churches. Bill took a job here with Rayonier Mill as a human resource manager while we were dating. I had no idea where the Olympic Peninsula was or anything else about it, for that matter.

During summer break while I visited my ex-in-laws in Long Beach, California, Bill had called me and asked if I would consider interrupting my vacation to fly to Port Angeles. He wanted me to check out a house he was considering buying. What a surprise! *Odd,* I had thought to myself. *Why would he want me to see this house?* His divorce had dragged on for over a year, leaving our future together in limbo. I knew I was crazy about him; nevertheless, it seemed there was much that needed to be taken care of before we could plan our future together. The conversation was awkward, explaining to Dad and Mom Hockel about the new man in my life and potential stepfather to their grandchildren.

I had been married to their eldest son, Louie, for nine turbulent years. I was eighteen, and he was twenty-one when we married, both of us very young. Mom's and Dad's faces had revealed their concern as they sent me off, albeit with their blessings.

The flight from Los Angeles to Seattle had been pleasantly smooth. The flight into Port Angeles on the small regional airplane was anything but smooth, igniting all my flying fears. *How am I going to get back to Long Beach?* I asked myself while gripping the armrests with each turbulent surge. Certainly not on this tiny puddle jumper!

When the small plane landed, I breathed a sigh of relief. Seeing Bill standing there had been enough…enough to remove the last awful minutes from my immediate focus. Together we made the short drive to the house on Tenth Street. "This is it!" Bill smiled with anticipation as he parked.

At first glance my impression had been positive. The house had a pleasant curb appeal—a neatly kept gray rambler embellished with bricks and a slightly winding walkway up to a small front porch. Bill opened the front door, and I stepped inside. Filled with curiosity, I quietly explored every detail as we toured the interior. It was a simple house, though nothing inside me had felt simple at that moment; a war of ambivalence churned as my fears and hopes met.

Did I dare get excited? Did I dare picture this house as home? Did I dare dream such a dream? Could I relinquish my fears and allow a space for my hopes and desires to take root?

Once outside the house, Bill and I had stood awkwardly on the front porch. Then, suddenly, he pulled me close to him.

"Will you marry me?" he asked gently.

Even though I'd waited and longed for this question, the weight of it bore down on me. This was a huge decision—not just for me, but for my children. I knew there are no absolutes and guarantees, but I had been willing to step out in faith…I'd been certain he would be a great father and husband. With only a brief hesitation, I answered him. "Yes!" At that moment, my concerns, worries, and fears vanished.

After my morning shower, I start a load of laundry and begin to think about preparing lunch for this afternoon. The nice thing about Port Angeles is everything is only fifteen minutes away. This geographic intimacy allows Bill to come home most days for a quick lunch. Although the time is brief, we cherish the rare moments of just the two of us.

After Bill's divorce was finalized, our marriage followed. On September 29, 1979, we said our I dos, and we moved to the house on Tenth Street in Port Angeles with my mother. Mom had multiple sclerosis and had lived in a nursing home near the house I rented in Bothell. There was never any question about moving her with us to Port Angeles. Bill and I had explored all the potential nursing homes in the city until the best one was chosen: Crestwood Manor.

The horrible disease had left its hideous mark on her at the young age of fifty-seven. She was confined to a wheelchair, and her memory had been impaired by the disease. She was confused about where her room was and often could not remember when she saw me last, even if it was only hours earlier. The unavoidable and uncomfortable time had come to obtain power of attorney over my mom. It wasn't a position I had wanted. What I had wanted was for Mom to be well and strong enough to make her own decisions. Sadly it didn't matter what I wished or wanted. MS had a different agenda. Mom's physical debilitation and rapid decline had made this legality necessary.

Going to church has always been an important part of our lives. After visiting every church in Port Angeles, we finally settled on the Assembly of God. Every Sunday we would pick Mom up from Crestwood Manor, and Bill would carefully move her from her wheelchair to our car. Once we arrived at church, he would repeat the transfer. Because Mom could not assist in any way, there were numerous close calls. Every once in a while, Bill would lose his grip and Mom would slowly slither through his legs, almost landing on the ground. The chaos turned comical and had us all in stitches. Mingled with laughter, she would frantically assert, "Bill, Bill, Bill!" Narrowly avoiding dumping her on the hard cement, he always managed to get her situated in the car, even if off-kilter, leaning to the right or left. The car was full of laughter the entire way to our destination.

After church Mom often came home with us for a home-cooked meal. It didn't matter what was served—it was certain to surpass the nursing home bill of fare. Pure pleasure covered her face while she slowly savored each bite like a little kid with a bowl of ice cream. Our family time together was precious, and my appreciation for Bill grew as I watched him lovingly care for Mom.

As I cut a crisp apple into slices, the tomato soup on the stove begins to simmer. It smells good. I hear the garage door open—my cue to start heating the grilled cheese sandwiches.

"Hi, Sweetie," Bill says as he greets me with a gentle kiss.

Bill is not a tall man, probably about five-eleven. He has broad shoulders, and something about being with him makes me feel safe. Early in our relationship, I was drawn to his love of nature and music. He played the clarinet beautifully and mastered "Just a Closer Walk with Thee" at my request. While at first I was concerned about our age difference, his vast life experiences enhanced our many long conversations and fed my longing for an intimate connection. He is a doer, a planner, a take-charge kind of man—something I will certainly enjoy getting used to.

While I finish preparing lunch, I hear him transfer the laundry I have started to the dryer and start the next load.

"Bill, come sit down, or this will get cold," I call to him.

We savor our alone time. He talks about driving up to Hurricane Ridge and showing the kids some of the hiking trails. He talks about all the chores he wants to do over the weekend—mowing the lawn and planting some African violets. I express my concerns about Travis and Heather and how they are adjusting to their new school. Bill reassures me that with time they will be fine. His confidence eases my worry. We talk about hanging some wallpaper in the dining room and going shopping for some new furniture.

"Really? A new dining room set?" I am delighted at the possibility.

We have so much to share during our lunch reprieves from children and business. It never seems like enough time. Reaching across the table, Bill opens my hand and writes with his finger, "I love you." This romantic gesture has become our special thing. The tenderness of his touch and the security I feel penetrate my heart.

But then our special moment is cut short. I don't know what I heard first, the phone ringing or Bill's voice.

"I'd better go, Sweetie."

Looking at Bill as I pick up the phone, I hope my eyes convey I want him to wait until I quickly end this call. I want to walk him to the car and say our goodbyes, just like we do every day. But the voice on the other end of the line pulls me back to attention. I don't recognize it.

"Mrs. Traub?"

"Yes?" I answer.

"This is Mary from Crestwood Manor. Your mom has a visitor, and we are concerned."

Without reason my pulse begins to quicken.

Mary, lowering her voice to a whisper, continues, "He reeks of alcohol."

My legs weaken from underneath as I find myself searching for a chair to support me. I'm unable to get one word out as the muscles in my neck and throat tighten.

"He is insisting on seeing your mother. Do you know who he might be?"

Oh, my God, no! It can't be him. *It just can't!*

Bill senses something is wrong. He stops his exit and sits back down in the chair. Finally I find words.

"What does he look like? Is he a big man?" I don't wait for an answer. "*Please*, don't let him…near her."

Everything in the room is swirling, and the muffled voice on the other end of the phone fades away. Bill takes the phone out of my hand.

"Let's get to the nursing home, Sweetie."

CHAPTER 2

Facing the Devil

The beautiful day filled with hope has vanished. A stream of images pulls my emotions in every direction. Like a soldier who returns to a horrific battlefield, my heart is pounding, my body weighed down with dread and apprehension while unsolicited memories begin to surface. Suddenly, without warning, I'm moved back in time. He is standing right next to my bed, breathing over me. The surreal images cast a dark shadow, producing chilling nausea and fear. I reach for Bill's hand.

Bill had already placed a call to Ted, our attorney. Ted, enjoying an afternoon flight in his Bonanza, responded right away and agreed to meet us at the nursing home.

Our usual parking spot near the front entrance of Crestwood Manor is vacant. I have walked through these doors so many times, visiting Mom often two or three times a day. *Will I have the courage to walk through them now?* I wonder. The two large doors seem daunting. Nevertheless, I move toward them, every step numbly joined to the next. Bill places his hand on the large wood door handle and tells me, "It's going to be okay." Usually Bill's calm, loving presence is enough to soothe my anxiety and fears, but not now. His words move *past me with no meaning or impact* and cannot quiet the fear rising within me as I move toward facing this wretched demon.

All I can think is that it has been years since I've been in the presence of this man. Years!

I do not know who painted the images in my memory. I do know the colors are vibrant and full of living, fearful moments of a child who is three and four and ten and twelve and sixteen. The images carry me back to a time when that child was powerless and unable to understand or protect herself. They carry me back to a time when survival meant finding a place to hide and wait, waiting for the enemy to enter my bedroom or call out my name. Now the enemy is on the other side of these two glass doors. Now I am no longer a child, and I must face him.

A gust of cold air sweeps past me as the doors open. Moving inside to the foyer, I try to shake off the cold and my nerves. To the right are two pink and burgundy floral wingback chairs. Florence, a dear sweet old lady, is sitting in one of the chairs. Her lips are bursting with unevenly placed bright red lipstick, her cheeks heavily dotted with pink rouge, her purse securely positioned on her lap. Most days when I visit Mom, Florence is sitting in this chair waiting and hoping someone will be stopping by to visit her.

As I usually do, I bend over and hug Florence. Just as I feel the warmth of our embrace, she sweetly whispers in my ear, "Hello, Dearie," and then an unavoidable sickening stench from the adjacent chair intrudes.

Unease mounting in my stomach, I turn and look. It's unfathomable! After all these years, he is sitting only a few feet away from me. Heavy, he fills the chair and reeks of cigarettes and alcohol. His head is slightly bowed, and I wonder if he is asleep. Or maybe he has passed! Could I be so lucky? Maybe we could just call an ambulance and have him removed. I notice the sleeves of his dark brown jacket are way too short, exposing several inches of his arms. Those arms! His arms send a cold, pulsing fear throughout my being. The buttons on his shirt are pulled taut, leaving openings exposing a dingy undershirt. I hold my breath because his putrid stench is leaching into the air I'm breathing.

A gentle touch on my shoulder from Ted interrupts my thoughts.

"Let's go over here," Ted tells us as he takes in the large figure sitting in the wingback chair. Ted ushers Bill and me into a small sitting room and tries to comfort me.

"Let me do the talking. Let me handle this," Ted speaks calmly. His words barely penetrate.

Suddenly a nurse's aide appears, pushing Mom into the small room in her wheelchair.

"No! She doesn't need to be here!" I plead to Ted.

Ted assures me it is the best thing and necessary. I have no resources to fight his strong position about Mom being with us. At the moment I feel powerless. I'm trying to handle my muddled, chaotic thoughts: *Why is he here? What does he want?* At the same time, I'm grateful Ted is with us to make decisions and take charge.

Mom's large brown eyes are locked on mine as if she is now the child looking to me for direction. Her face is thin, frail, and childlike. She's not the gutsy mom I remember. I see her worry and concern, and I certainly feel a responsibility to protect her. Does she know he is here?

Ted steps out of the room and returns with the slow-moving, heavyset man. He pulls up a chair and motions for him to have a seat.

Ted initiates the conversation. "How can we help you, Mr. Milbrandt?"

The response is slow and slurred. "Well, I need Blanche to sign these papers."

Sign what papers? I wonder.

Something unexplainable compels me to look at him square in the face. He looks decades older than the last time I saw him. My heart races, and beads of sweat collect on the palms of my hands. His face is red and puffy. His nose is bulbous, covered with broken blood vessels, and his eyes are so much smaller than I remember. They're barely open, it seems. His horrendous stink is overwhelming in the small room. I reach over and take Mom's hand.

"Blanche, just sign these damn papers. What's the deal? We've had a joint checking account for years. I need to sell the house," he grumbles.

Ted's response is quick and clear. "Blanche is not signing any papers. Kathy has power of attorney for Blanche, and as her attorney, I can tell you no papers will be signed."

"Blanche, come on, sign these papers. Let's go—I'll take you home."

Mom's eyes continue to be locked on mine…never moving even with his lurid commands. Unsteady, he rises from the chair, moving toward Mom. Louder, he plants his last effort.

"This is bullshit, Blanche. Just sign the goddamn papers!"

Without thought, I place myself between the two of them, standing face to face with the devil. I have moved into a new space, a space of power. I look straight into his bleary eyes, and with years of seething contempt, I shout, "I am not signing any papers. We are done here!"

Turning away from him, I grip the handles on Mom's wheelchair, navigating her out the door. Like a small child fearing the repercussions of being defiant, I hurriedly push Mom the short distance down the hallway to her room.

"Are you okay?" I ask her. Her brown eyes reveal her unease. Yet she nods yes.

I fill her glass with fresh cold water and sit with her for a few minutes. Then, still shaking, I head back down the hall, where I find Bill and Ted talking.

"Oh, Ted, thank you! I'm so glad that is over and you were here with us."

Ted offers me his hand. "Yes, I'm glad that is over for all of you."

Strangely I feel utterly exhausted, shaken, and simultaneously exhilarated. While every word of the brief encounter replays in my mind, I feel brave and confident. I just stood face to face with evil, and I didn't run! I didn't hide! I'm not that child, not that little girl anymore!

After a few deep breaths, I walk back to Mom's room. As my hand hovers over the doorknob to her room, I find it odd the door is closed. Her door is rarely closed. I instinctively know something is not right. Cautiously I turn the knob and push the door open. I am bowled over by what I see.

Like a vampire sucking the life out of its victim, his mouth is wildly pressed against her lips. Her arms stretch up to him while his are tightly wrapped around her frail body. Stunned, I feel a flood of emotions pour through me. Slowly I back out of the room and brace myself against a wall. Tears do not come. Chaos swirls in my mind as I try to find my breath.

The bold, victorious feelings I felt only minutes earlier seem to vaporize into the wall supporting me. Only a shadow of myself is left, a small, trembling, blond-haired girl, wailing inside.

Why, Mom? Why?

CHAPTER 3

Styrofoam Cup and a Six-Pack of Beer–1965

I watch the clock closely. It is three thirty in the afternoon, and I have about thirty minutes. Rummaging through piles of clothes on my bedroom floor, I spot some jean cutoffs, then scramble to find my crumpled-up sweatshirt underneath my bed. I grab it and pull it over my head.

For a minute I lie back down on my bed, fighting an overwhelming need to crawl under my blankets for a little longer. But I know I can't. Mom will be home from work soon, and I can't let her know I didn't go to school. I can't let her know I haven't been to school in maybe two weeks. Days have muddled together; I've lost count of exactly how much school I've missed. One thing I do know is that I'm failing most of my sophomore classes.

Making my way to the bathroom, I search for a hairbrush. Behind the cupboard door, there is the one with the white handle. With four girls in the house, hairbrushes are difficult to come by. A big "M" painted with bright red fingernail polish is Mom's remedy for letting us know this brush belongs to her. I pull the brush through my long blond hair, add a little hair spray, and I'm done. Now I can go back, lie on my bed, and listen for her car to pull into the driveway. Drawing my blanket over my body, I wait.

Before long I hear her car door shut, and shortly after I hear the front door open. Paying close attention, I hear Mom going through her usual routine: setting things down on the kitchen counter and cracking open a can of beer. I can't avoid her any longer.

I make my way to the hall outside my bedroom and observe her in the kitchen. She is dressed in her unvarying white uniform, and her thin, chestnut-brown hair is pulled back in a French roll. Only the faint remnants of red lipstick remain on her lips. She smiles briefly when she sees me. Today her big brown eyes tell me she is in a good mood. The starched brown-and-white-checkered apron she wears as part of her Hof's Hut uniform has already been shed. Her girdle and nylons are draped over a chair. Everyone she works with calls her Sam, and the nickname has stuck with her. Even my friends recognize her as Sam.

As she does every day, she makes herself comfortable at the kitchen table. On the table sits an ashtray, a can of Coors beer, and a Styrofoam cup. The small white Styrofoam cup contains nickels, dimes, and quarters—the tips she earned today.

"Hi, Mom," I say as I pull out a chair and join her at the table.

At first Mom is quiet. Slowly she shares a little about her day as she turns the Styrofoam cup upside down and begins separating the coins. I know her job is demanding. The odor of food and hard work pervades the room. For the most part, Mom enjoys the people she works with. Occasionally she shares stories about work and the shenanigans they pull on each other.

Today, with a grin covering her face, she shares a funny story with me.

"Like usual, I met the delivery man at the back-door entrance. You know, over the years he's gotten to know me pretty well. He gave me a wink, understanding I was up to some sort of 'no good.' Then he handed me the large container of eggs. I winked back and promised to leave him out of the entire affair." Mom's eyes widen a bit as she shares with me.

"Oh my gosh, Mom! What did you do with them?"

"Well, I took them in the back and glued all the damn eggs in place. I mean they wouldn't budge. During the flurry of the breakfast hour, the cook, George—you remember George... he quickly grabbed an egg, and it wouldn't move. It was glued tight! He grabbed another before he finally caught on and realized not one of them was moving."

Both of us laughing, Mom takes a drag off her cigarette and continues...

"The entire tray was full of shattered eggs, and George was ticked off! I just meandered around doing my job, waiting on my customers. But I could hear him swearing like a sailor! Of course, I'm no dummy. He'll be looking for the opportunity to get back at me!"

Mom and I have a good belly laugh. She takes a sip of beer, and I continue sorting the quarters. Sharing the story with me, the laughter momentarily diminishes the fatigue on her face.

I start stacking quarters in groups of four. Fortunately stacking the coins helps her and is a diversion for me. One beer is gone. She asks me to get her a second as she lights another cigarette. As the coins are stacked, they are eventually loaded into paper wrappers. When just the right number of coins are loaded into a wrapper, the paper ends are bent and twisted to secure the roll. Mom places the completed rolls off to the side.

While we sit around the table, our conversation is easy. It is a huge relief she hasn't asked me about school because I don't know what I would tell her. As Mom places the wrapped roll of coins off to the side, my thoughts wander.

I remember the day she gave me a green roll of dimes equaling five dollars. Mom sent me to Hiram's grocery store to get a half gallon of milk. But as I approached the grocery store on my bike, I quickly got distracted. The parking lot was completely full, and people were walking in all directions. A large multicolored sign, CINNAMON SUGAR PRETZELS, grabbed my attention.

A small carnival had unexpectedly set up residence in the parking lot. I set my bike down, captivated by the large Ferris wheel, bumper cars, the enticing aroma of cotton candy, and the exuberant laughter that filled the air. I couldn't resist and began wandering curiously through the noisy crowd.

It was the goldfish game that apprehended my attention. A little money and a fishing pole with a magnet on the end of the line would allow me the opportunity to take home one of those tiny, enticing orange fish. It couldn't be too hard! After all, I only wanted one. All I had to do was fetch a small toy set between numerous small bowls that held the adorable sought-after tiny orange fish.

Excited and determined, I edged my way up to the counter, unraveled the bent end of the green roll, and carefully pulled out a few dimes. My first go at the fishing game was over in a matter of seconds. Refusing defeat, I gave it a second, third, and fourth try. Before long the wrapped coins had diminished to nothing. In only twenty minutes, the dimes were gone. Discouraged, I returned the fishing pole empty-handed—no goldfish, no money, and no milk. I felt like the biggest loser in the world, and I knew I was in big trouble.

Riding my bike home that day with no money or milk, I had conjured up stories…Maybe I dropped the roll of dimes and lost them, or maybe somebody robbed me. A week following my carnival episode, Mom arrived home from work a little later than usual. Before settling into her normal routine at the kitchen table, she gently deposited a round glass bowl on the counter. Inside, dashing about, was one tiny orange goldfish. No words were exchanged between us, but her big brown eyes conveyed all I needed, and my enormous smile gave away my gratitude and elation.

Sitting with Mom today, stuffing a green paper roll with dimes, I glance over at the glass bowl holding my tiny treasured goldfish, and I'm reminded of how hard she works. A rush of shame comes over me as I reminisce about wasting the money she works so hard for.

Finally we are finished. Mom seems more relaxed and is enjoying a third can of Coors. I plant myself onto her lap and snuggle my head against her shoulder. For a few moments, I feel warm and content. Like a baby bird nestled safely in its nest, I yearn to be close to her.

"Okay, Katy Sue, get up. I swear you girls will want to sit on my lap when you're thirty years old."

"Of course we will, Mom! We will never be too old to sit on your lap."

Oh, how I want to linger here close to her. I treasure the brief closeness as a gentle push coaxes me off her lap.

Mom gathers up the rolled coins and places them in a cupboard. Later they will be used to pay bills. Draping a freshly cleaned and starched apron over a white uniform, she begins the routine for tomorrow. Mom hangs the clean uniform on the knob of a closet door in the hallway. She is ready for another day of work.

As she often does, she settles in on the living room sofa. Eventually she stretches out on her stomach and falls asleep. A couple of hours will pass until she finally stirs and makes her way to her bedroom for the night. The six-pack of beer is gone, and the Styrofoam cup is empty, waiting to be filled with tomorrow's tips.

CHAPTER 4

Caught in Evil's Chasm

Silence fills the car as Bill and I head back home. "I have a few things to button up at work, and then I will come right home," he tells me.

Shaken and trembling, I frantically plead, "No! You can't go back to work! Please! He is going to come kill us! I'm telling you he is! You have to believe me!"

Once we arrive home, Bill makes a short call to work and then sits next to me on the sofa. We begin to talk through the possible scenarios. Will he leave today? Will he go straight to a bar? Bill suggests we drive to the airport and inquire about the flights leaving Port Angeles today. Surely his name will be on one of them. His idea brings me a tiny bit of relief.

My blissful morning full of beautiful joy has plummeted. Now I'm drowning in fear. I don't want this evil infiltrating my happiness, our future! He has already stolen enough from me! I need reassurance this horrifying demon is leaving—leaving this town, my home…far away from my family.

Bill stands holding my sweater in place as I slip into it. But its warmth doesn't ease my shaking. We climb into our car and begin the short distance to the airport. The blaring radio grates on my raw nerves.

"*Please*, Bill, can you turn it off?" I bark at him.

I reach over and touch Bill's hand. "I'm sorry for being so harsh—my nerves are raw."

Finally we are there. He pulls into an empty spot and parks. "Do you want to come in with me?" he asks.

"I don't know. No! No! I don't want to see him," I respond.

I wait in the car silently, keeping my eyes glued to Bill as he enters the small Port Angeles regional airport. The smell of jet fuel and the clatter of luggage wheels bumping against the cement are minor distractions from the weight of my thoughts.

It isn't long before I see Bill returning toward our car, nodding at me. The news is good!

"His name is on the four o'clock flight out of PA," Bill informs me.

Four o'clock is a couple of hours from now. I ask Bill if we can wait.

"I need to see him leave. I know it doesn't sound rational, but I need to see him walk into this airport and leave this city."

So we sit, and we wait.

Four o'clock comes, and we have not noticed anyone resembling him. Realizing my unease, Bill goes back to the terminal to inquire about the scheduled passenger, Mr. Donald Milbrandt. The clerk at the counter tells him, "The plane has boarded and is scheduled to take off soon. Mr. Milbrandt is not on the flight."

"When is the next flight?" Bill inquires.

"There is one more flight out at seven o'clock," she replies.

It is a given we will wait. We will wait to be assured he boards the next flight and will leave our world, hopefully forever. But Donald Milbrandt does not board the last flight out of Port Angeles. Bill and I drive the short distance home.

Once home I rush into the house to check on Travis and Heather. They are fine. They are oblivious to the anxiety and fear overwhelming me. Where could he be? Where did he go? Is he parked on a barstool in one of the taverns or passed out somewhere? Is he plotting an act of vengeance for his failed attempt to get Mom's signature?

As soon as the kids are in bed for the night, I pace through the house, allowing all the possible scenarios to run through my mind. Occasionally I peek out a window, looking for what, I'm not entirely sure—an unusual car parked outside, someone walking around our house? Nothing is escaping my imagination. Eventually Bill persuades me to come to bed.

"He is going to come kill us!" I implore.

A tsunami of fear swirls in my stomach, producing waves of nausea as I sit upright against the headboard of our bed.

"He is going to come kill us!" Exhausted, I let my words fade away.

* * *

I desperately want to grab my sister's hand. We are sitting only inches apart, but I can't reach her. My frantic desire to help my sister is futile. Terror grips every muscle in my being, paralyzing me. Then I feel it, cold, hard, pressed against my head. I scrunch my eyes tight and wait...

* * *

"Good morning, Sweetheart," Bill says, gently pressing his lips against my head.

CHAPTER 5

Father's Day 1950

I t is Sunday, June 18, 1950.

In only a few hours, the sun will peek above the horizon, and homes throughout America will start preparations for the day's festivities. Children will awaken to add proud finishing touches to crafty homemade cards and eagerly assist their moms in preparing scrumptious breakfasts of biscuits, gravy, crisp bacon, fresh eggs, and homemade cinnamon rolls. Families will gather in backyards or neighborhood parks around the enticing aromas of barbecues to honor and celebrate the special men in their lives. Today is Father's Day!

For twenty-nine-year-old Blanche Leone Kluck, a host of emotions overwhelm her on this early Sunday morning. She checked into Centinela Hospital Medical Center in Inglewood, California, a little past midnight after enduring several hours of intense labor at home. She quickly kissed the foreheads of her daughters, whom she left sleeping comfortably in their beds. Nine-year-old Janice Lee and two-year-old Christine Ann are unaware the baby their mommy has been carrying in her tummy is about to join their family.

Soon she is settled into room 206 in the maternity ward where the atmosphere is sterile and chilly. Nurses come in and out, attending to Blanche and one other lady also in vigorous labor. A thin white cotton curtain hanging between their beds provides a slim veil of privacy and yet fails to hush the anguish of labor. A simple silver round clock is hung over the doorway. It reads 4:36 a.m. Unfortunately the cries from the lady on the other side of the white curtain are unnerving and impossible to ignore.

Frightened tears begin to roll down Blanche's face as she tries to bear the harsh contractions now coming every couple of minutes with less and less relief. She wonders if this baby will be the perfect Father's Day gift, the boy her husband, Harold, has always wanted. One of the nurses wipes the perspiration from Blanche's forehead with a cold, damp cloth and gently tries to encourage her. Waves of nausea make things worse. Blanche has been so consumed with her pain that she hasn't noticed that the lady next to her is no longer in the room. She has probably been taken to the delivery room, Blanche reasons.

Nearly unbearable, the pain reaches a crescendo as Blanche's tummy constricts with each harsh contraction. She looks up at the clock, which now reads 5:05 a.m. The nurses quietly converse before summoning Dr. Nealy. After a quick examination, Dr. Nealy sets everyone in motion to move Blanche to the delivery room. Swiftly her bed is pushed into a room bright and cold. Nurses draped in long surgical gowns, white caps, and masks hurriedly move about the room. Everyone has designated tasks he or she is responsible for. Turning her head from left to right, Blanche takes in the commotion surrounding her. A slight sense of relief soothes her fears, hoping the excruciating pain will soon be over. One of the nurses standing near her head urges her to push with all the energy she can muster.

"Push! Push! Just one more time. Push!"

Amazingly and wonderfully, on June 18, 1950, at 5:42 a.m., a six-pound, seven-ounce newborn baby girl receives a firm pat on her soft, wrinkled bottom. Without hesitation the newborn's loud cry confirms her entrance into the world. A united celebratory chatter fills the hospital delivery room just as the cry escapes the new baby girl. The birth process and adjusting to life outside the womb are a huge transition. This newborn baby girl has been thrust from the snug and dark womb where the comforting, steady sound of her mommy's heartbeat has been a constant. Soon the baby's lifeline, the umbilical cord, is severed. For the first time, she is breathing completely separated from her mother. Within minutes the nurses quickly attend to the sweet little girl: suctioning her nose, placing drops in her eyes, and wrapping her gently in a white cloth. At the same time, Dr. Nealy is busy finishing the last surgical procedures that go with childbirth.

The cold, bright room is filled with excited anticipation of uniting mother and baby for the first time. One of the nurses gently places the newly wrapped bundle next to Blanche's side. Utterly exhausted, Blanche turns her head away from her new baby. With no energy left to pretend even a tiny bit that she is excited or happy, she tearfully orders the nurse, "Take her away! Please, take her away."

The sun had risen, and it is shaping up to be a gorgeous summer day. The hospital staff is immersed in all the usual morning goings-on. Now back in her room, Blanche has slept off and on all morning, occasionally interrupted by nurses taking her vital signs and softly chatting among themselves. Blanche had heard it all.

"Maybe today will be better after she gets some rest," one nurse had speculated.

Even though she practically just finished running a marathon, a breakfast tray delivered doesn't look one bit appetizing—whole wheat toast, scrambled eggs, cold cereal, and a small carton of milk. Blanche has zero appetite. Alone in her room, she pushes the breakfast tray aside with the weight of despair consuming her.

The day ends, Monday, June 19, begins, and still Blanche has not seen her baby. The nurses have tried several times to talk to her, but she remains distant and unyielding, refusing to see the baby girl.

Nonetheless, there is some important legal business to attend to: the baby's birth certificate. Dressed in black slacks and a floral summer blouse, a woman from hospital administration enters Blanche's room. She isn't interested in the new mother's mental state. She is completely focused on the business at hand. All the usual questions to legally document the newborn's birth are asked: mother's name, age, and address—Blanche Leone Kluck, twenty-nine—father's name, age, and occupation—Harold Emil Kluck, thirty years old, milkman. The woman peers at Blanche over her clipboard and asks, "What is the baby's name?"

Blanche is silent. Finally, through a cloak of sadness, she replies, "Kathryn Sue."

A pen and the document are set in front of her. Her signature is required to verify the accuracy of the information.

Blanche has been in the hospital for five days. Overwhelmed with gloom and hopelessness, she has not been able to move even one step toward embracing her newest child. The staff on duty have mentioned they haven't noticed the baby's father being around. Concerned, one of the doctors on duty asks the hospital chaplain to visit with her.

A short, stocky man with eyes full of kindness arrives to visit the new mom in room 206. His mission is to cheer her up, make some sense of her behavior, and hopefully propel her in the right direction. He chats with Blanche for about an hour. Before he leaves he asks her if he can pray for her. Blanche nods.

Five more days go by. Ten days after the birth of Kathryn Sue, Blanche gives the go-ahead for the nurses to bring the baby girl to her. Earlier that day her own mother arrived from South Dakota. A no-nonsense woman with a sturdy gait and an air of authority, Bada Dartt had marched into her daughter's room in the hospital and read her the riot act.

"Shape up now! This baby is going to bring you joy like you've never known!"

Maybe it was ten long days in the hospital, or a fierce scolding from her mother, or possibly a short heartfelt prayer that jarred Blanche and softened her heart. She might never know what finally prompted her to embrace her child.

Finally, on the tenth day, Kathryn Sue and Blanche are united and will soon be on their way home.

Hearts Like Wildflowers

I hope you are blessed
with a heart like a wildflower
Strong enough to rise again
after being trampled upon,
tough enough to weather
the worst of the summer storms,
and able to grow and flourish
even in the most broken places

Nikita Gill

CHAPTER 6

New Beginnings 1939

Today is a big day, a milestone! Harold mulls over the significance, standing in front of the mirror in the small family bathroom. He squeezes a dab of Brylcreem into his palm and rubs his hands together. Massaging the pomade through his fingers, he slicks his hair back to achieve a sleek, dapper look. Turning his head a little to the left and then to the right, he looks himself over in the mirror.

Standing five feet eight inches with wavy brown hair, grayish-blue eyes, and dimples, he is a good-looking young man, and he knows it. Lean and athletic, he is active in basketball and football. His friends dubbed him Bulldozer. Even though his height hinders him, his stature doesn't stop him from being a force to be reckoned with. All his buddies have a healthy respect for him, understanding he is not one to back down from any confrontation. Puffing out his chest and

flexing his muscles, he lingers in the bathroom, admiring himself in the mirror. *Not bad,* he thinks to himself.

"Are you still alive in there? You're going to be late for your own graduation!" Harold's father says as he raps firmly on the bathroom door.

"Oh shit!" Harold grumbles. He looks at the clock, realizing he told Blanche he would pick her up for their ceremonies five minutes ago.

Harold Emil Kluck, born on January 31, 1920, and Blanche Leone Dartt, born the following year on April 21, 1921, are the quintessential small-town boy and small-town girl. They both spent their youth on the rural farmlands in Browns County, South Dakota. They come from formidable stock, parents who survived the lean years of the Great Depression and the hardships of the Dust Bowl, and whose values are rooted in hard work, determination, and family. True grit and tenacity are embedded in their bones. It is no surprise that Holly, the name she sweetly assigned him, and Blanche fell in love and had big dreams together. And it is no surprise their peers voted the handsome couple King and Queen of Columbia High School.

In the family station wagon, Harold screeches up to the front of Blanche's home.

"Oh Lord, I'm in trouble," he mumbles to himself as he sees her waiting on the front stoop.

Blanche, a tall, slender, natural beauty with chestnut-brown hair and striking large brown eyes, inherited her mother's strong-minded temperament, creating her own force to be reckoned with. Blanche never lacks in speaking her mind. Holly had learned early on he could read Blanche's immediate disposition through her big brown eyes. Today he can already see he is the cause of her piercing, fiery glare.

"You are ten minutes late, Holly!" Blanche blurts out as she climbs into the station wagon. "I imagine you'll be late for your own funeral!" she continues.

The day's warm sunlight glistens on Blanche's tight face. Holly often finds her stunning beauty, mingled with her fiery temperament, enticing. Even through her jabs, he can't ignore the fluttering in his chest.

"You take my breath away, Blanche Leone!" he says sweetly.

As Blanche's beauty redirects his attention, Holly realizes just the sight of her has brought the little soldier under his trousers to full attention. He leans toward Blanche to give her a kiss. Swiftly a playful whack on his arm rebukes his affection.

"The King and Queen of Columbia High School shouldn't be late to their own damn graduation party!" she bellows, and off they drive to be officially crowned.

* * *

When Blanche isn't helping her dad and mom at their small family café, she is with Holly. Whenever the two of them can break away from family chores and responsibilities, they venture off alone.

"Let's go, Beautiful," Holly instructs as he tosses Blanche's packed lunch and other goodies into the back of the station wagon, ready to head out to their favorite fishing spot, Alkali Lake.

Steering with his left hand, Harold places his right hand on her leg while they make the short, scenic drive to the lake.

Life doesn't get much sweeter than this, he muses to himself. At last, they reach the secluded, bumpy dirt road they had happened upon last summer. After being tossed about, they finally reach the end of the road. They like to believe this perfect hidden gem is a spot known only to them.

Harold backs the station wagon right up to the lake's edge and lets down the tailgate. Blanche takes a deep breath, inhaling the fresh, warm air. She is awed by the landscape surrounding them, covered with small, delicate, white and purple Hesperis wildflowers. While Blanche lays out a blanket on the edge of the tailgate, organizing their lunch, Holly grabs his favorite fishing pole.

"Maybe I'll catch another one like last summer," he reminisces with Blanche about the largemouth bass he caught. "That six-pound catch was some of the best fish I've ever eaten," he proudly asserts.

After some fishing and wolfing down lunch, Blanche surprises Holly and brings out two cans of Reading beer she'd snuck out of her parents' cafe.

Snuggled together, dangling their legs off the tailgate and sipping their beer, Harold asks, "So now that we have graduated and are truly adults, when do you want to get married?"

Blanche turns her face toward Holly and places a big kiss on his cheek. "I'm ready, Mr. Kluck! I'm ready to be all yours!"

The two of them crawl into the back of the station wagon and cuddle for several hours, daydreaming about the promises their future holds.

And so on July 25, 1939, nineteen-year-old Holly and eighteen-year-old Blanche are united in marriage. Mildred,

Holly's sister, stands next to Blanche, and her husband, Gerald, stands with Holly.

It is a small, simple, and perfect ceremony. Blanche's brown hair, in soft curls, frames her face beautifully. She wears a flowy white ankle-length dress with delicate short capped sleeves. A white lace bow is gracefully draped around her beautiful bouquet of coneflowers and white Lenten roses.

Standing straight and proud next to his beautiful bride, Holly wears a handsome tailored off-white suit. A crisp white shirt and a dark tie, embellished with a tie pin his father had given him, complete his attire.

With a few special friends and both their families surrounding them, they face each other, holding hands and softly expressing their vows. Blanche stands before Holly with her eyes closed, collecting herself and savoring the moment. She takes a deep breath, and any tension she felt seems to vanish.

"I love you, Holly, and I promise to love you today, tomorrow, and always."

Harold's eyes fill up as he listens to her every word while looking into her big brown eyes. And then he responds.

"I promise to love you, I promise to care for you, and I promise…to always be on time."

Everyone bursts into laughter, including Blanche.

The sweet ceremony comes to a close, and the celebration begins. Mr. and Mrs. Harold Kluck, brimming with joy and high hopes, truly feel like a king and queen on their wedding day. They are deeply in love and ready to face the world and all the new beginnings to come.

Uncle Ozzie, Grandpa Kluck, Harold, Blanche,
Grandma Kluck, Aunt Mill

CHAPTER 7

California Bound

Unable to cast off the bothersome nudge stirring inside of him, Harold sits down on the edge of the sofa, pulls his boots on, and ties the laces.

"I'm going down to the lake for a bit. I need to do some thinking," he hollers out to Blanche, who is outside hanging some freshly laundered bed linens on the clothesline.

Blanche stops what she is doing for a moment and listens to Harold through the open kitchen window. She isn't surprised. She has noticed Harold hasn't been himself lately.

Harold hops into his truck and drives the short distance to their favorite spot next to the lake. *What the hell is bugging me?* he wonders. *My life has been perfect since marrying Blanche,* he continues to ponder while standing on the grassy edge of the beautiful lake.

"What the hell? What is wrong?" he shouts out into the universe.

Harold picks up a handful of large pebbles. He scours the bunch, looking for the biggest, flattest rocks, and one by one, sidearms them over the water. The first few rocks land with a big splash, but finally a rock bounces three or more times before disappearing into the water. The simple game of skipping rocks stirs up a host of his fondest childhood memories. He treasures the memories when his dad would break away from chores on the farm and spend time alone with him.

Damn, I remember when Dad taught me how to bait my first hook, me trying to hold onto that slimy worm. He taught me how to cast out my own line and reel in my first catch. We sat and waited for hours before I felt that nibble. So many memories move through his thoughts. *It was my dad who taught me the value of patience and sticking with it. It was my dad who taught me how to pick the right rock and, after a million tries, how to get it to gently skip over the water.*

After an hour or so, Harold's mind returns to the present. *There just has to be more.* The nagging voice in his head is relentless. Suddenly a possible clue surfaces.

He learned the value of hard work and patience from his dad, but he also saw his dad's efforts devastated by the dusty plains of South Dakota. He watched how hard his parents worked, only to have their lives turned upside down by economic hardships. There must be more than the toil of working land taunted by drought and scorching winds. Harold can't still the restlessness plaguing him.

I want something different. No matter what it takes, I'm determined to seek a better life. Harold makes up his mind and quickly drives home to tell Blanche. They decide on a plan in which Blanche's brother will go with him—to be safe, yes, but for his own gain too. The two will seek a new life and brighter future outside of South Dakota. Once they find it, Blanche will join them.

Feeling exuberant, Holly kisses Blanche goodbye. Blanche is swimming in a mixture of emotions—sadness, fear, and excitement—but she will say nothing to stanch Harold's excitement.

She tucks two cans of beans, smoked pork jerky, and several pieces of bread and butter into his knapsack.

"I'll contact you as soon as I can," he promises.

She places both of her hands on Holly's face and stares into his eyes. "Be safe, and take care of my brother."

Layered in shirts and an old wool sweater, with two dollars and sixty-eight cents in his pocket, he is ready for the adventure of his life.

Bud, Blanche's younger brother, and Harold walk out the front door and thumb their way to Aberdeen. Harold had attentively listened to all the rumors and figured the best time to avoid being spotted was during the dark hours of the night. So in the wee, hazy hours after midnight, Harold and Bud find the switchyard where they plan to jump onto a freight train with the Milwaukee Railroad. The freight train is heading west…California bound.

In the dark of the night, Harold bounds onto an empty boxcar and then hoists Bud up. Together they hunker down in the corner of the car, not wanting to be discovered. It isn't long before the whistle sounds, and a great spur of steam fills the night sky. The train begins to move—slowly at first—with a gradual gain in momentum. Bud is like the little brother Harold always wanted, and he feels a heavy weight of responsibility to protect him. He also knows Blanche will have his head if anything happens to her baby brother. Huddled together, side by side, adrenaline pumping through them, their nerves are raw. But the exhilaration they feel for what is ahead surpasses their fears.

Within minutes the train begins to pick up speed. As it does, the wooden floor creaks and tosses them up and down.

Eventually, after they are pitched about for several hours, exhaustion gets the best of them. Bud passes out first, his head resting on Harold's shoulder. Not long after, Harold drifts off. The train roars into the night, oblivious of the two freeloaders moving further and further away from things familiar.

The night sky begins shifting as the rising sun peers through the darkness. A cold wind blows into the boxcar as the bluish dawn hints of a new day. Awake and chilled to the bone, Harold and Bud shiver in silence. The train pulls into Rapid City at daybreak.

"It's time to hit the road," Harold murmurs to Bud as he nudges him.

Taking a quick look outside the boxcar, Harold jumps first with Bud behind him. Row after row of trains fill the switchyard. Harold had heard stories about one of these trains heading south to Cheyenne, Wyoming. He had been instructed that after Cheyenne the next leg of the journey would be to hop a boxcar to Salt Lake City, Utah. From Salt Lake, they would make the last trek to Sacramento, California—California, the land of promise.

At this moment, the call of nature can't be ignored any longer. Both of them desperately need to find a place to relieve themselves. Walking between cars, they notice small bushes about one hundred feet beyond the trains where they won't be detected. Taking turns standing guard, they are each able to take care of business.

Next the two men plod through the freight yard. As luck would have it, they overhear two workers talking.

"Which train is heading to Cheyenne? Foreman Ray said a brake coupling needs to be looked at."

The other man raises his arm, motioning in the direction of a line of boxcars three tracks over. "It's over there. You better hurry. It's leaving in two hours."

Trying to blend in, Harold and Bud cautiously follow the brakeman as the activity in the yard ramps up.

In the early-morning hours, workers at the switchyard are occupied attending to various jobs: greasing axles, loading boxcars, staging trains, and refueling. Cautiously Harold and Bud find an out-of-the-way boxcar and climb in.

Hungry, they ration out a little of the food they brought along and settle in. Every once in a while, they hear workers outside the boxcar. Neither moves or makes a sound. Harold had heard all the horrible stories of hobos tracked down by railroad detectives and, without any right to protest, forcibly removed from the boxcars. Other stories told of men jumping from the moving cars, never to be seen again, and still other rumors mentioned men losing fingers snapped off by boxcar doors. These stories haunt him.

Tired and weighed down with uncertainty, Harold wrestles with his thoughts of what he left behind and what he hopes is ahead of him. And during the four grueling, long days it takes to get to Sacramento, Harold has time to do nothing but think.

When the train finally begins to slow down as it approaches Sacramento, Harold and Bud decide to jump from the boxcar rather than risk being discovered. Together they leap from the moving boxcar. Dirty, worn out, and a little bruised, Harold and Bud walk miles to some open farmlands where they find an irrigation canal, dress down, and wash off four days of stink. Drying off in the scorch of the day, the two of them double over in laughter, recalling some of the best parts of their long, nerve-racking journey.

Captivated by the rich organic smells of the fertile fields that dominate the landscape surrounding them, Harold stretches out on his back in the grass, mulling over what they have undertaken. They have done it!

Satisfaction swells within him, and he is convinced he can tackle any challenge he might encounter. He has made it this far, and nothing will get in the way of his ambitions. The two men have come over one thousand miles closer to their dreams of prosperity.

CHAPTER 8

Prosperity, a Double-Edged Sword

The phone rings once, twice, and then a third time. Blanche scurries as fast as she can from the bathroom, where she had just finished showering, and grabs the phone in the kitchen… she does not want to miss the call.

"Hello?" she answers, trying to catch her breath.

"Hi, Beautiful!" Instantly she recognizes Holly's voice, and her heart flutters as an unrestrained surge of relief washes over her. The relief transforms to warm tears that flow down her cheeks.

"Hi, Holly! I miss you so much. How is Buddy? Are you both okay? Where are you?" With no pauses, the words fly out of her mouth.

"Slow down, Beautiful. We are finally in Sacramento, and we are both fine. I can't talk for long. I put all my change into this phone, and I'm not sure how much time it gives us. I've got good news! I've landed a job at a dairy farm, and Bud has a job roofing. So start packing, Blanche."

They talk for a few minutes before the line inevitably cuts out.

Blanche hangs up the phone and breathes in deep lungfuls of air. *California, our new home,* she thinks to herself, wiping tears from her face as a wide grin spreads across her lips. She would follow him to the West Coast soon enough.

43

* * *

Work on the dairy farm begins before the sun rises. Harold works from sunup to sundown, shoveling cow manure, cleaning barns, feeding livestock, milking cows, and doing whatever else he is told to do.

He and a few other hired hands had been given a cot in the bunkhouse and fed two meals a day as part of their pay. Under his bunk bed, he had hidden a glass milk bottle. Every penny he earns is stuffed into the bottle for safekeeping. But there is one exception: drinking money. At the end of a long day, he is willing to spend some of his hard-earned bucks for a few beers with the guys.

Hungover from the previous night's drinking spree, Harold has a swirling stomach. As luck would have it, the one and only latrine is occupied! Rushing outside he bends over and heaves the contents of his stomach onto the dirt. Momentarily he feels a little relief.

"Way to go, Harold! Do you even remember us dumping you in the back of the truck to get you home?" his buddies chide him.

"You might be a hard-ass worker, but you are a candy-ass drinker!" The loud laughter rubs against his raw nerves.

Harold sits at the end of his bunk, grabs the glass milk bottle, and pushes the remaining change from last night's escapades into the hole. *What a waste of money,* he thinks to himself. But it won't stop him from repeating the same old mistakes.

Harold has developed a reputation not only for being a good drinking buddy who doesn't know when to stop, but also for being a hard worker. And his hard work hasn't gone unnoticed.

After six months, old man Verburg offered Harold a job he couldn't refuse—his own milk route in Gardena.

Harold turns the milk bottle upside down and draws out some change to call Blanche. "Pack your suitcase, Blanche! Verberg gave me my own milk route!" Harold shares the news with his beautiful wife, whom he misses terribly. Soon they will be together.

Distinguished in a white Verberg milk truck, and a white uniform, including a cap and bow tie, Harold bursts with pride. Having his own milk route is a long-awaited change from the dirty jobs he had been used to. He personalizes each delivery by memorizing family names and noting small details. The Milkman, as he is known, is well liked for leaving the family dog biscuits alongside the glass milk bottles he leaves on the front porch.

Soon the glass milk bottle holding his life savings grows to four bottles, then five, and then six. His hard work is paying off. The timing is perfect: Blanche is due in September to give birth to their first child. Now that Harold is going to be a daddy, he wants to avoid the draft and war. On July 1, 1941, he enlists in the United States Army.

Janice Lee is born on September 14, 1941, a precious bundle of innocence. Harold is over the moon and in love with his new daughter. Janice Lee is daddy's little girl and her mother's pride and joy.

After months and months of hard work, Harold has a big surprise. "Look, Blanche, we have enough money for a down payment on the house we want." The house, selling for $3,250, is an enormous undertaking. *I'm up for the challenge*, Harold thinks, singing his own praises.

The charming white bungalow in Gardena is more than they could have ever hoped for: two bedrooms, one bath, a good-sized kitchen, and a small covered front porch. In the front of the house is an area with flower beds and luscious green Bermuda grass. In the rear of the house is a detached garage that includes a cozy apartment with its own entrance. It feels like they are jumping off a huge cliff with no guarantee they will land on their feet.

Life is good for the three of them, with lots of money coming in and the purchase of their first home. However, all the successes begin to have another impact.

Prosperity seems to be a double-edged sword.

With his milk route done for the day, Harold pulls into the parking lot of the Alondra. *Just a couple of beers,* he thinks to himself. But one beer leads to another, and soon a couple of hours have passed.

Hanging out with good buddies goes clear back to his high school days. He finds a certain freedom in it that he often craves after his long workdays. He has always enjoyed the comradery—talking sports, playing a game or two of pool, and sometimes, after a few too many beers, letting his guard down and occasionally getting marriage struggles off his chest. The problem is that he never watches the clock or considers the family and dinner waiting for him.

"Oh, crap! I'm in trouble!" Harold hollers over the spirited music of Glen Miller's "Chattanooga Choo Choo." He does his own exaggerated choo choo past his drinking chums, waves goodbye, and exits the bar.

Blanche sits at the kitchen table stewing. She has already put Janice down for bed. Two plates of cold dinner sit in front of her. *How could he be so inconsiderate?* she asks herself.

Cautiously Harold walks into the kitchen, trying to read Blanche's temperament. Clenching her teeth and fighting back tears, Blanche picks up both plates and deposits them in the kitchen sink. A little tipsy, Harold smacks her on the butt as she walks past him.

"It's okay, Beautiful—you probably could go without a few meals…that's not all leftover baby fat!"

Then all hell breaks loose.

Harold makes his way to the sofa and passes out. Blanche retreats to their bedroom, slamming the door behind her. It isn't the first time Harold's cutting comments about her pregnancy weight gain have moved her to tears, and she knows it won't be the last.

Then, unexpectedly, their lives are turned upside down.

"Harold! Harold!" Blanche franticly blurts out. "Come here…hurry. Please!"

Harold enters Janice's bedroom and sees Blanche's ashen white face. In her crib Janice lies listless, burning up with a fever.

"Come on—let's get her to the emergency room." Harold's quivering voice sets an avalanche of fear in motion. Shaking, Blanche wraps her lifeless daughter in a blanket. Once outside, Harold opens the car door and helps Blanche in, and off they drive for help.

It had been sudden. High fever and weakness had overtaken her little body. Doctors break the devastating news: their sweet little girl has rheumatic fever, and she might not survive. The doctor's words bear into Blanche: "If she does survive, enjoy every minute with her; she will not have a long life."

Harold and Blanche sit motionless, absorbing the doctor's words. Although Janice is small, she is brave and fierce, and she fights for her life and survives.

* * *

Janice is a very slender little girl, at all times adorned in special beautiful homemade dresses. The doctor's words always loom in the back of Harold's and Blanche's minds. It makes sense that they are very protective parents, and yet simultaneously they expect near perfection from her. Good manners are a must—please and thank you, yes ma'am and no sir. She learns to play the piano beautifully but is not allowed to participate in sports. Asthma often overpowers her, a side effect of the harsh rheumatic fever. Janice Lee is the center of their world for seven years, until in late 1947, after several miscarriages, Blanche learns she is pregnant with their second child.

Harold proposes an idea. "Blanche, what do you think about adding another bedroom? Our family is growing, and we have the money."

"Well, I imagine we will need the extra space." Blanche thinks adding a bedroom is a great idea.

At the same time, Harold's Uncle Richard and Aunt Annie fall on hard times. Uncle Richard is struggling. He has been out of work for months. Harold offers his aunt and uncle the apartment attached to their garage until they can get back on their feet. *This is a real bonus!* Harold reasons to himself. His cousin Don, a roofer by trade, lives with his mom and dad and can help with the construction of the new bedroom. It seems like a win-win for everyone, and Harold's cousin Don will add another drinking buddy.

One morning Blanche walks along the flower garden on the far side of their yard and waves good morning to the crew working on the new addition. Making herself comfortable in a lawn chair, she welcomes the sun's warmth against her face. Placing her hand on her tummy, she gently caresses the life growing inside of her. It is nearing the end of May, and her baby is due in August. She watches pillows of white clouds move across the sky and wonders about the future…the arguing, the drinking, and now a new baby.

Drinking after work has become Harold's normal routine. Recently she has noticed the mean streak in Harold return, and it makes her uneasy. Blanche doesn't feel safe. *He pushed me hard enough to make me fall. And I'm pregnant!* she reflects. *He is ashamed of how big I am when I'm pregnant. And he is jealous of everyone…especially Don.* Layers and layers of thoughts hold a dark cloud over what should be a special time in her life.

A month passes, and Blanche is planning a family Fourth of July get-together. She hasn't been sleeping well at night. Her baby has dropped, causing cramping in her pelvis and thighs. She wonders how she is going to lug herself around for another month when she is out of breath just getting up off the sofa.

Grocery list in hand, she wants to get the shopping done early, before the heat of the afternoon sun.

"You look exhausted…but still beautiful," Don says with a smile, standing right outside her kitchen door.

"Just don't say I look fat, and you're as safe as anyone can be around me these days. And you're right. I'm tired and grouchy and on my way to the store," Blanche responds sharply.

"Let me take you. They don't need me here for a little while." Worn out and grumpy, Blanche can't refuse his offer.

The shopping list is easy: hamburger, hamburger buns, corn on the cob, and store-bought potato salad. She has already determined she isn't making her own potato salad, even if it is Harold's favorite. Don runs to the beverage aisle and grabs beer and sodas, and they are done.

"I'll drive, and let me take you for a quick lunch," Don says, moving into the driver's seat.

Blanche only hesitates for a moment. These days she is always hungry. "Okay—after all, I am feeding two."

"And you are beautiful."

Blanche takes notice—this is the second time he has called her beautiful, and it certainly feels good.

Driving back home after lunch, Don reaches over and puts his hand on Blanche's leg. "I want you to know I'm always here for you. My cousin should really appreciate what he has and treat you right."

Blanche wonders if Don and his parents have heard their loud arguments. It sure seems that Don knows something is not right.

Later that night Harold arrives home late as usual. Blanche isn't even bothered. She has thought about Don's compliments all afternoon, which gave her a boost in confidence and joy. *Who cares if he is late?* she thinks to herself as he enters the kitchen. Soon it is obvious Harold is in a heightened state of agitation. He begins his usual badgering.

"Who would want to be seen with you? Look how fat you are!" he barks at her.

Finally she has had enough. Bursting into tears, she blurts out, "Don thinks I'm beautiful!"

Before she can catch a breath, Harold rushes out the door straight to the apartment at the rear of their house. Blanche follows, grabbing Janice's hand when she realizes her daughter has witnessed the entire argument.

Brash yelling and cursing from both men fill the backyard. "You stay away from my wife!" Harold shouts, taking a wild swing at his cousin, his fist connecting with the side of Don's face.

The two throw punches at each other until Don pulls Harold to the ground and holds him down. "You better start treating her better, or I'll take her off your hands," Don yells while holding Harold down.

Harold thrashes about, throwing punches at Don. Finally his rage dissipates, and the two men separate. After this violent encounter, the hostility between the two men is palpable. There is no love lost between them.

A month later, on Monday, August 2, 1948, Christine Anne is born after thirty hours of labor. She isn't the boy her Daddy had hoped for. Nonetheless, born with a full head of dark brown hair and big brown eyes like her mother, she is precious and loved.

Janice Lee is overjoyed to finally have a baby sister. When Christine arrives home, Janice does her best to contain her seven-year-old exuberance and carefully cradles her tiny baby sister. Filled with excitement, Janice insists if her neighborhood friends want even a glimpse of her new baby sister, a gift is required. Janice is certain her baby sister deserves presents and lots of them. After all, she had prayed for a baby sister for some time.

August and September are hot and dry. The yards in the neighborhood need extra attention, or they will turn a scorched brown. Blanche is a busy mom, trying to tackle all the household responsibilities—shopping, preparing meals, laundry, keeping the house tidy, and keeping up with two children.

The kids had been up for a few hours, and Harold had left for work before the sun rose. Blanche walks through the kitchen and looks at last night's cold dinner still sitting on the kitchen table. Opening the fridge, she pushes containers of leftovers around to make a spot for the two plates. *This is what he gets tonight if he comes home late again!* She feels a rush of resentment brewing inside her. She walks through the living room—picking up dirty tissues, a half-empty cup, and unopened mail—then trips over her shoes in the middle of the room. Tears well up in her eyes. Bitterness and resentment have taken up residence in her heart. *I don't want to do this anymore* is the thought tumbling through her mind at that moment. Feeling overwhelming loneliness and less and less emotionally connected to Harold, she reasons, *We have zero meaningful conversations. Heck, I barely see him. He doesn't make us a priority at all anymore. His drinking buddies are more important. He takes me for granted and is only happy as long as I cook a hot meal and have the house clean. Why am I even here?* she wonders.

Peeking through the living room windows, the morning sun catches her attention. She steps out into her yard. Being outside with the sun's warmth on her face is healing and productive. Tending to her flowers, she unravels the hose and turns the nozzle on. Once outside, she breathes in the fresh air, and slowly her mood shifts. In the back of Blanche's mind, she secretly hopes Don might notice her and come outside for a chat. Don is one person who makes her feel alive and happy. Hoping to see him, she lingers, over watering her flowers. Then she realizes Don's truck isn't there. *He isn't coming out.* She turns and wraps the hose up.

As the months pass, the tension between Harold and Blanche does not diminish. Arguing, drinking, and conflict become the norm. Blanche takes a waitressing job in the evenings at Dell's. Maybe her new job is an escape from the turmoil and duties at home. The new attention she receives from patrons puts a bandage over her loneliness and eases the unhappiness she wrestles with.

Blanche's commitment to her marriage is unraveling. Her heart isn't fully in it anymore. The late hours she puts in at work mean she is even more tired and distracted. They mean she relies on Janice to help with housework and tending to Christine. They mean Harold is even more jealous and accusatory.

Harold's cousin Don, keenly aware of the growing crack in Blanche and Harold's marriage, continues to show up to help at just the right moments. Blanche is vulnerable to his every attention.

Unsavory rumors begin to circulate that Harold has also found other places to devote his interests. Finally the rumors reach Blanche. There had been subtle signs—his anger and lack of interest in her, his coming home later and later—but Blanche hadn't wanted to believe them.

It is rapidly becoming evident prosperity hadn't been enough. All the monetary gains and what they provided have done nothing more than take their eyes off the love that once united them. If anything, the "good life" has brought about changes that seem to produce an indulgence in things with temporary pleasures. The two of them, who had once been so devoted to each other, grow further and further apart. Then, amid tremendous turmoil, in November 1949, a huge surprise leaps into their lives again—another pregnancy.

A new baby is to arrive in June. And whispered rumors swirl... *Who is the father?*

CHAPTER 9

Hush, Little Baby

The thirty-minute drive home from the hospital is completely silent. Kathryn Sue, wrapped in a swaddle blanket and securely held in her grandmother's arms, sleeps peacefully. Blanche, apprehensive, anticipates her mother's stern rebuke for being unwilling to embrace her new baby, but enduring her mother's silence is worse. *What is she thinking about me? How could she possibly understand?* she wonders to herself. She needs her mother's support more than ever; however, she knows Bada Dartt is not one to compromise her values or convictions or be silent about them. Blanche decides to keep her problems to herself, well-guarded.

Two weeks pass, and it is time for Bada to return home to South Dakota. She has been a tremendous help in caring for her grandchildren, cooking and attending to the household chores, while Blanche regained her footing after childbirth. With her heart feeling heavy and her mind moving in a thousand directions, Bada neatly folds her freshly laundered clothes and lays them in her suitcase.

Next, Bada rummages through the bathroom, gathering up her toiletries. *How could their marriage get so off track?* she asks herself. It isn't the tension in the home that troubles her most, but something worse: the lack of love, joy, and commitment. Harold seems indifferent toward his family. Bada's concerns are justified as Blanche is barely managing to go through the motions of motherhood. It is obvious their marriage is in trouble, and the children are paying a big price.

Bada shakes her head in frustration and glances at her watch. It is time to go. She hates leaving her grandbabies. She has big concerns she cannot silence. *How will their drinking and arguing impact the children? Will they continue to stay out late and expect Janice to tend to these babies? I wish they would get it together before it's too late.* With a heavy heart, she stoops down, wraps her arms around them, and pulls them in close against her large bosoms.

"Be good for your mommy and daddy, and remember I love you." Heartbroken, she swallows the tears welling up in her throat and believes the only thing she can do is pray for all of them.

* * *

One morning in December, Blanche notices Kathy doesn't seem like herself. The eighteen-month-old is lethargic, her head extremely warm. Concerned, Blanche yells out to Janice to come sit with her sister while she hunts down the thermometer.

"Where is it? Where is it?" she shouts, turning drawers inside out while her intuitive mother's instinct brews inside.

Something is wrong…seriously wrong! The thermometer reads over 105 degrees. Immediately Blanche picks up the phone to contact her doctor.

"Put her in an ice tub" are the instructions on the other end of the phone. Janice, who often takes on the mommy role, scurries about the kitchen. She empties all the ice trays into a large bowl and brings the cubes to her mom. Blanche, leaning over the tub, dumps the entire bowl of ice into the water and drapes cold washcloths on Kathy's chest and face. Soon, after the ice bath, they rush out the door to take Kathy to the hospital. Her temperature would not drop.

As soon as the admitting staff in the ER see the little girl, they rush her back, and nurses begin to scurry around. A young doctor arrives in the small room as an IV is started, and one of the nurses takes Kathy's temperature. Blanche can tell by the nurse's face it isn't good—107 degrees. The doctor places a stethoscope against the little girl's chest. He immediately orders a chest X-ray. Wailing, Kathy is whisked off without her mother. Blanche feels like a tight rope is tied around her chest. A heavy despair weighs down on her as she reflects about rejecting Kathy at birth. *Could this be my punishment? Is my child getting sick what I deserve?* Silently she pleads, *No, God, no… please don't let anything happen to her.*

The forty-five minutes she sits alone feel like hours. Her mother's words plague her. *This baby is going to bring you joy like you've never known.*

"Your little girl is very sick. She has double pneumonia. Both of her lungs are full of fluid. We are admitting her and will let you know what room she is in as soon as possible." The young doctor's words are piercing.

Blanche sits up straight as if someone has jolted her with a hot poker. Finally she is given the room number, and with her heart racing, she immediately makes her way to the elevator and third floor. When she enters the room, two nurses are standing around the hospital crib that holds her daughter. She can barely see Kathy's face as some sort of mask covers it. There are multiple tubes; one feeds intravenous antibiotics into her small arm. She squeezes in next to one of the nurses, picks up her daughter's tiny hand, and gently strokes it. Tears well up in her eyes as the realization of how sick Kathy is hits her. Silently she pleads with God to please make her daughter better. Later it is determined her little girl is anemic and will need blood through an intravenous line to replace the missing red blood cells.

Managing everything at home and overwhelmed with worry, Blanche makes the drive to the hospital a couple of times a day, visiting her daughter for several hours. On more than one occasion, she is enraged when she changes Kathy's diaper and discovers blood from a horrible diaper rash. *How could they let this happen?*

For the first several days, her little girl is listless and sleeps a lot. Sometimes her little body trembles as if she is cold, but the nurses will not allow any blankets and insist on no clothing except her diaper. Finally, her fever begins to come down, and as it does she is more awake and aware. The visits are painful. Little eighteen-month-old Kathy cries out in a frenzy when her Mommy leaves her sight. Blanche has to leave—she has Janice and Christine at home.

Three weeks of hospitalization and a flood of antibiotics later, it is determined Kathy can go home. The hospital stay has had a very adverse effect on the little girl. The impact begins to show up through rageful tantrums, sometimes lasting for forty-five minutes or until she exhausts herself. Separation from her mother seems to be the trigger that ignites one of her outbursts. Screaming, crying, and thrashing about, Kathy works herself into a fury. As the energy in her little body dissipates, she curls up on the floor, gasping and gasping until she finally falls asleep.

It is wonderful to have everyone together at home, but it also heightens the reality of how far apart Harold and Blanche have become. He keeps late hours, and Blanche carries the load at home, exhausted from everything she has on her plate.

Two weeks after Kathy comes home from the hospital, Blanche is called into work for a day shift. One of the other waitresses had a death in the family. The timing is horrific, but she feels a burden to help out because others had been willing to cover her shifts while she was at the hospital. Now she has to figure out who will tend to the girls. She knows Harold can't miss the deliveries on his milk route, and Janice is at school. With no one else she can think of, she picks up the phone.

"Don, I'm so glad I caught you. I've been called into work, and I'm looking for someone to sit with the girls. Janice will be home from school around three o'clock, and she can take over then. You've always said if I ever needed anything…" She didn't care about potential repercussions from Harold—she just didn't care anymore.

Knocking on the back-door kitchen entrance, Don arrives about ten minutes early. Six years younger than Blanche, about six feet, two inches, lean, and very muscular, he is dressed in jeans and a white T-shirt. Common for roofers, his arms and face are well tanned. She always feels a little flustered when she is around him and begins to ramble.

"This caught me completely off guard…I hope it isn't ruining your day. Thank you for helping me out."

Smiling at each other, they hold a longer-than-usual gaze. *He is so handsome*, she thinks to herself. She makes him a cup of coffee and begins to go down the list she had prepared detailing instructions about eating times and naps and different activities to keep the girls entertained.

"Both girls will go down for a nap around…" As she reads from the list, Don moves closer, interrupting her thoughts.

"Don! I'm trying to give you some help here!" She says with a smile.

Ready to go, Blanche grabs her purse and thanks him for stepping in and helping out. Kathy had become very reactive whenever she saw her mommy pick up her purse. Don had previously witnessed one of her tantrums and swiftly picks Kathy up, determined to short-circuit any misbehaving. This only makes things worse. Instantly Kathy begins screaming. With tears running down her cheeks, she stretches her arms out to her mommy. Blanche leans in to console her baby girl, but Don blocks her with his forearm and sternly barks, "Leave now! She will be fine!"

Blanche, startled by his loud command, stands still for a moment. Turning her wrist to see the time on her watch, she can't ignore the pull to get to work on time and tries to reason with herself that he might be right. Finally, she dashes out the front door.

Don, face flushed red with impatience, immediately sits Kathy down on the floor, where her outburst escalates. As she screams and hits her head against the floor, he still ignores her. Christine crouches down, trying to comfort her baby sister. Cup of coffee in hand, Don moves to the sofa in the living room.

Little Christine walks from the kitchen, where her sister thrashes about on the floor, to the living room, where Don thumbs through the newspaper.

"Baby cry, baby cry," she murmurs.

Don ignores her. Distressed, Christine's little legs travel back and forth from the kitchen to the living room, from the living room to the kitchen. Suddenly Don springs up. Abruptly he grabs Kathy up from the floor. Carrying her into the bathroom, he leans over the bathtub and turns the shower on cold. Kathy continues to wail, her back arched as he places her in the bottom of the tub with cold water pouring down on her. She flails around screaming, cheeks bright red and tears streaming down her face. Her emotional outburst continues for more than twenty minutes, until she finally exhausts herself and lies trembling at the bottom of the tub. Cold water continues to drench her, and her screaming turns into deep sobs as she searches for air.

Hoisting her up by her arm, Don pulls her out of the tub and carries her into her bedroom, depositing her on the floor. Christine follows right behind him. He leaves her on the floor and closes the door behind him. Dripping wet, shivering, and panting short, shallow breaths, she curls up on the floor and eventually falls asleep.

"Hi, Mom," Janice calls out as she walks through the front door from school at exactly 3:10 p.m. She sees Don and instantly feels unsettled. *What is he doing here?* she wonders. She had told her mom she didn't like him one bit but hadn't told her why.

She will never forget. It was a warm summer afternoon. Mom and Dad barbecued hamburgers in the backyard. Uncle Richard, Aunt Annie, and Don had come over. Everyone was having fun, telling stories, and laughing. It was all fine until it was time for them to go. Uncle Richard and Aunt Annie each hugged her goodbye. But then Don leaned over, kissed her on the lips, and pushed his tongue into her mouth. Then he pulled away.

"Goodbye, Janice," he said with a grin on his face.

She had wanted to throw up. She had hurried to the bathroom and hung her head over the sink, gagging. She wiped the inside of her mouth out, spitting over and over. She was afraid to tell anyone. After the awful fight she had seen between her dad and Don, she didn't dare. She didn't want any more fighting or her Daddy getting hurt.

Now feeling very apprehensive, she avoids him as she walks around the house looking for her sisters. She finds both Christine and Kathy asleep in their bedrooms. Feeling uneasy, she quietly goes into the room she shares with Christine and closes and locks the door behind her. She waits, hoping her mom will be home soon.

It isn't long, and she hears the back door slam shut. While her little sister is fast asleep in her bed, she cautiously peeks between the blinds in the bedroom window and watches Don walk away. She is thankful he is gone. Anxious, she goes to the kitchen, locks the back door, and exhales a big sigh of relief.

CHAPTER 10

Long Beach, California

Blanche understands her marriage had died long before the actual divorce. Slowly she had begun to grasp the notion that things weren't going to change. The ups and downs had gone on too long, resulting in loss of trust and loss of intimacy and ultimately diminishing the sweet love she and Holly once held. She deals with the pain in bite-size pieces, and, though hard to face, the reality is her dreams of a beautiful life with Holly have come to an end. Still, she longs to be loved and happy. And the one person who continually shows up, Harold's cousin Don, has left her with the hope she could still realize her dreams of a happy forever.

With Blanche's divorce finalized, the two rush off to Las Vegas and tie the knot. Her share of the community property from the divorce provides the down payment for the brand-new rambler on Carfax Avenue.

Pointing and gesturing, Don guides the truck driver attempting to back into the long driveway. A loud, high-pitched tongue whistle is intended to alert the driver his back tire is cutting into the newly planted fescue grass. Hanging his head out the cab window, the driver quickly reacts and blurts, "Oh, shit." He adjusts with a sharp turn, but the wheel sinks deeper into the fresh sod.

Meanwhile, Don is tired and pissed off. It has been a busy week signing final mortgage papers and getting the keys to the new house in Long Beach. A squinted glare and a few harsh words directed at the driver convey his annoyance.

With three bedrooms, one bath, and a nice kitchen, everything in the house sparkles. Blanche takes in a deep breath, savoring the distinct fresh smell of newness. Mentally she has already assigned bedrooms and knows precisely where each piece of furniture will be placed.

Five-year-old Christine and three-year-old Kathy will share a bedroom, and Janice, now almost a teenager, will have her own. Blanche is keenly aware this move will be the hardest on Janice, who is very attached to her daddy. There is no question; she is her daddy's girl. What's more, Janice has made it known she doesn't like Don one bit. Blanche hopes giving Janice her own bedroom will cushion the transition.

Both bedrooms face the street side of the house. A short hallway off the bedrooms includes a linen-broom closet and a door into the bathroom. At the end of the hallway is Don and Blanche's bedroom. Wood paneled and wallpapered, the cozy living room in the center of the house separates the bedrooms from the kitchen. In the kitchen a large window over the sink looks out onto the front porch, and in the back portion of the kitchen, a door opens onto the driveway and a full-size detached garage.

Blanche, thrilled for this new start, directs the movers as they carefully carry in labeled boxes and larger pieces of furniture. Christine and Kathy run through the empty house, giggling with excitement. Watching anxiously, Janice stands back out of the way waiting. Finally her massive upright piano is carefully carried into Christine and Kathy's new bedroom and placed against the only wall wide enough to accommodate it. This makes the bedroom very tight, especially when the full-size bed is brought in and placed snugly against the opposite wall. Janice breathes a sigh of relief, and slowly the house fills up with furniture, eliminating the echoing sound of emptiness.

It isn't long before Blanche takes a waitressing job at a small family restaurant, Grisingers, about fifteen minutes from their newly established neighborhood. This gives her some income and helps with the transition into her new life but also means she sometimes has to leave the girls at home in Don's care. The girls don't like their mom being away. Don rules with a fiery temper. If Kathy has temper tantrums, cold showers are his favored remedy. Janice and Christine hang close together, avoiding him as much as they can.

Long Beach is now home to the five of them. Cubberley Elementary and John Marshall Junior High are all within walking distance, which is ideal for the girls. Reports have it a new high school is to be built nearby in the next couple of years. In addition, Hiram's grocery store is also a couple of blocks away, making for an easy walk or bike ride. The new homes in this residential area sell quickly. Carfax is bursting with young families and new beginnings.

* * *

The late summer afternoon is warm and breezy in the suburbs of Long Beach. Blanche sits in a lawn chair, and Christine and Kathy run around on the front lawn, making silly nonsensical singing noises and laughing. Suddenly three more children appear, two boys and a girl—Mike, Stevie, and Dana, neighborhood kids who live across the street. Then two more kids join in, Anita and Janice, who live in another house across the street.

"We came over to see if you wanted to play," says Mike, a young boy. And just like that, the kids fold into a little troop and slip into a boisterous game of chase.

Over the following years, the neighborhood friends offer something special: a protective space where children are free to laugh and play and flourish. Some of these childhood friendships will develop into beautiful bonds that create a lifetime of memories.

CHAPTER 11

Streetlights On

So many memories of my childhood friends are forever etched in my mind—the simple, naive, yet meaningful kind of stuff that secures splintered parts together through a special bond found in friendships. There were pinky swears, poking fingers till blood was drawn and merged in a blood pact, and sharing secret codes and heart-to-hearts while walking to and from school. We hollered secret messages to each other from our bedroom windows well after our bedtimes. "Eee-ahh-kee!" we yelled, until suddenly our bedroom lights went on and a harsh "It's time to get to sleep" ensued. Blankets draped over clotheslines gave stage to backyard carnivals and talent shows, until Mom arrived home from work and furiously dragged her linens back inside for washing. For certain I will never forget the neighborhood friends I grew up with on Carfax.

In the warm summer days and nights of Long Beach, we spent endless hours playing games outside until the streetlight came on, illuminating the street and sidewalks. Regardless of any unspoken turmoil within our homes, fun, love, acceptance, and trust anchored our childhood bonds, providing a respite through the ups and downs we experienced growing up.

Spacious, our front lawn was the perfect place. Kids came from both ends of the block and often brought friends from adjacent neighborhoods. We congregated on the grass, giggling and ready to play.

"I want to be Mother!" several voices yell out.

"No, you were it last time."

And so it goes until finally someone rises to the forefront and claims the lead of Mother in the game "Mother May I?"

Charlotte proudly takes the lead spot today. She is one year older than me and lives in the house behind us. For us, getting together to play is easy. We just hop the six-foot wood fence that separates our houses, and back and forth we go. I can never get enough time at her house. Her mom is often at the stove cooking something yummy that stirs all my hunger pains. Charlotte's father, Jack, built Charlotte every girl's perfect dream playhouse. It is so much fun to play in her playhouse and eat a big bowl of her mother Velma's delicious homemade macaroni and cheese.

Charlotte's brown eyes hold a unique sparkle. Jack and Velma Stratton adopted Charlotte when she was an infant. She is their only child, and they spare nothing to make her feel loved and happy. Their love and kindness often spill over to my sister and me. "Come with us!" With a big smile, Jack would include us in trips to the beach, Knott's Berry Farm, and even Disneyland.

Today the game of "Mother May I?" has started. Directing all of us to move to the far end of the lawn, Charlotte puts a huge distance between herself and the rest of us.

Karen yells out, "Mother, may I take ten jumps toward you?"

Charlotte yells back, "No! Mother says, 'You can take five steps toward me.'"

Karen responds, taking five of the largest jumps her thin little legs can produce. The idea is to get closer and closer to the goal of touching Mother. All of us yell out whatever we can think of to bring us closer to tagging Mother. "Mother, may I take two spins and four leaps?" "Mother, may I crawl five feet?"

Mike Qualls, known to show off a bit, yells, "Can I do five cartwheels?"

In unison everyone begins to laugh! Mike forgot to say, "Mother, may I?" and now he has to go all the way back to the start line. Several hours drift away on our front lawn yelling "Mother, may I?" and laughing until someone finally reaches Charlotte and tags Mother. Eventually, a few friends meander off for home, and then a few more, but for certain they will be back another day for more fun.

My sisters, Janice and Christine, are known for creating magnificent French rolls and beehive hairdos. At the crack of dawn, on school picture day, many young ladies from the neighborhood gather and wait in line for perfected hairdos. Lots and lots of Aqua Net hairspray and a rat-tail comb with the long, pointed end are essential for the perfect result. Everyone understands a little dirty is best and are instructed not to wash their hair for at least two days prior—preferably three for the perfect outcome. One by one they take the chair in front of the mirror in our living room. Janice and Christine, already adorned with the magnificent 'dos, have gotten up extra early—makeup on and hair done.

As the girls sit perfectly still in front of the mirror, the creation of the bouffant coiffure begins. First the hair is parted and backcombed. Some of the girls grimace as the rat-tail comb works its magic. "Hold your breath," is the repeated warning as endless amounts of hairspray provide the lacquered hold. Ratted and sprayed over and over, the hair is folded, and bobby pins are strategically placed. The thin pointed end of the rat-tail comb is creatively used to pull the hair up, fashioning volume, and the other end of the comb is used to create the smooth elegance. The updo is magnificent. On this early morning, the yawn-bearing young neighborhood ladies sit up straight with joy decorating their faces. They feel beautiful! Christine and Janice finish by applying a little makeup on their young, flawless faces—sometimes more than their parents are happy with.

I am in third grade, eight years old, when my sisters graciously adorn me with one of their artistic masterpieces for school pictures. The enormous bouffant must add five inches to my height. Of course, their finishing touch of bold winged black eyeliner is the icing on the cake. I walk to school with my head held high, touting tremendous pride. Soaking in the numerous stares with cast-iron certainty, I believe someday I might be on the cover of one of those *Glamour* magazines my sisters salivate over.

As I settle in at my small metal-and-wood desk, whispers permeate the classroom. Mrs. Haynes, waving her hand, motions for me to come forward to her desk. Stiff-necked because I'm not used to the enormous pile on my head, I approach her with a huge smile.

She quietly asks me, "Did your mother approve of your beautiful hairdo and makeup? You are sure to stand out in the yearbook."

And stand out I did! My mom is stunned when the class photos arrive. There I was, in print, truly "larger" than life.

My sisters have the gift of working magic with the rat-tail comb and Aqua Net hairspray. Their talents produce a lot of confidence, smiles, and a special sisterhood among the girls in our neighborhood.

* * *

When dark descends upon Carfax, the streetlight, situated right across the street from our house, keeps all of us neighborhood kids in line. In the late afternoon, when the day's heat begins to diminish, we gather at the streetlight for a game of hide-and-seek. The game is very popular with our gang.

Stevie Qualls is chosen to be "It." His head resting against the wood trunk of the streetlight, eyes closed, he loudly and slowly counts to twenty-five. Dashing about, the rest of us quickly hunt for a place to hide. We only have twenty-five seconds to find our spot. Our hiding places vary from under a nearby car, or behind a bush, or snuggled around a corner between houses.

"Ready or not, here I come!" Stevie yells.

This is our cue to hunker down in silence and watch. Suddenly, Mike runs across the street and hits the wood streetlight post, yelling out, "Olly olly oxen free!"

To the far left of me, I can see Stevie has found Anita and is making every effort to tag her. Jumping back and forth, she dodges his touch until finally she makes it to the pole. "Oxen free!"

Stevie turns and begins his search again. Squatting behind a hibiscus bush, I make my run for the pole. *Whew!* Out of breath, I tag the pole. "Free!" At the same time, I hear Stevie yell out, "Tag! You're it!"

His exuberance fills the air as he swats Christine with his hand. Laughing and out of breath, Christine surrenders and takes her place at the streetlight for another round of hide-and-seek. Eyes closed she begins to count to twenty-five.

After several games the sun's radiance dims as it slowly sinks into the horizon. Ignoring the inevitable approaching darkness, all of us kids gather together for one more game of hide-and-seek.

Darkness continues to fill the sky unapologetically. Then on cue, as if they were kindred spirits, the streetlight responds to the darkness and spreads its light over the street on Carfax. The streetlight we had leaned our heads upon in play is now telling us it is time to go home. This is the instruction set by many parents in our neighborhood: when the streetlight comes on, get home!

Sweaty and wound up, we honor the streetlight's silent glowing command. A few hugs are exchanged as we say our goodbyes and retreat to our homes.

For me, the play time together provides a respite, free of worry and unease—a safe harbor from the secrets I carry.

Ready or not, time to go home. The streetlight is on.

CHAPTER 12

Terrors in the Night

Home can be a dreadful place. Every day I'm afraid of what will happen when Don comes home. I've learned if he has too much to drink, he is really mean, and if he only has a few beers, he is too friendly. When he walks through the door from work, I take in everything around me. My eyes and ears become radar antennae. On high alert, with adrenaline coursing through my body, I can figure out what kind of mood he is in and how the terrors of the night might unfold by his smell and his tone of voice.

Tonight, it's late, ten o'clock. Christine and I crawl into the full-size bed we share. Fussing and adjusting the covers, my sister settles in against the wall. I stretch out, straightening my legs, trying to get comfortable. Tired, we both know the rule. The imaginary line between us is not to be crossed—the "don't touch me" line. I scoot over to the invisible line, moving as far away from the edge of the bed as I can. Finally, sleep comes to both of us.

For a time the night is peaceful. Dreams of furry pets at play and favorite superpowers dancing freely travel through a kaleidoscope of sleeping visions. Even as a young child, I understand slumber provides a time when I can let go of weighty burdens, when my little body is nourished and can rest and grow. Slumber feels like a holy time, a time when guardian angels come to visit and whisper while wrapping their soft feathered wings of protection around me. These revered angels have special ways of warding off lurking shadows and fears of darkness, bringing me peaceful slumber and rest.

But then an uninvited, intrusive heaviness enters the room and clashes with the good, disturbing the sacred space where I sleep.

I can smell him—alcohol and cigarettes. I can hear him—his breathing is heavy. Through slitted eyes, I see a large figure standing over me. I know it is him.

Lying rigid as a statue, I wait. I command my eyes to close tightly. Maybe tonight he will turn away and leave. Sometimes he does that. Sometimes he just stands next to our bed and does nothing. As he stands there, the stink of him fills my nose and thickens in my throat. The blanket covering me is a thin protection. I want to pull it up over my head and hide, but I can't move—fear won't let me. A pull on the blanket makes my heart pound fiercely in my ears and throat. Fumbling around, his big, heavy, rough hand scrapes against my tummy.

I hate him touching me!

I am frozen. I lie silently, screaming inside without a voice, LEAVE ME ALONE! I HATE YOU! LEAVE ME ALONE! while his large, rough hand makes its way under my panties, exploring me, hurting me.

He is gone, but his violent intrusion into my body lingers. I pull my legs up to my chest, curling up tightly. I wish I could disappear. Why didn't I yell at him to stop? Is my sister asleep? I hope she didn't hear him. I don't want her to know. I remember the night I begged her to let me sleep against the wall. She wasn't happy about it, but she agreed. I heard him come in that night. I could smell him. I could feel the blankets moving about. Did he hurt her too? That night I pressed myself against the wall with my back to my sister and lay in silence, waiting for him to leave. I did nothing to help her. I should have been sleeping on that side of the bed.

Sometimes sleeping in the closet is our escape from his nightly visits. Sometimes after my sister falls asleep, if she hasn't already escaped to the closet, I climb out of bed and curl up on the floor in the small space. Toys and shoes are strewn about; I make my bed atop them. It isn't the most comfortable with toys poking into my back and side, but I curl up anyway. Without a blanket for warmth, I shiver until I fall asleep. Some nights I don't hear him come in. Other nights when I do hear him, I keep silent, hoping my sister will cling to the wall and escape his reach, being the only one in bed available for him to…

One morning Mom finds me asleep in the closet. "What the heck is Kathy doing sleeping in the closet?"

Christine quickly answers, "Don won't leave us alone! He keeps coming into our bedroom at night and watches us in the bathroom!"

Mom's eyes widen with anger. She follows Christine to the linen-broom closet in the hallway and opens the door. A small, dime-size hole has been cut out, exposing anyone on the other side, in the bathroom. Mom grabs some tissue and scrunches it into the hole. Then she paints her red fingernail polish over it. That day she goes to the store and buys a lock. She screws the small lock in place on the inside of our bedroom door. A small latch-type lock is certain to provide us with safety. Or at least that's what we think before the next evening settles.

A loud boom wakes Christine and me. Startled, we spring up, leaning on each other. Then the room turns silent except for our own fearful breathing. Dazed, we can see him in the doorway. One swift kick, and our protection is gone. He turns and walks away. Later the tissue filling the peephole in the linen closet disappears. These will be the last protections provided for us.

Some nights when Mom is away at work, Don yells out one of our names, "Kathy, Kathy, come here."

Instantaneously my fear of him clashes with my hate for him. Fear always wins out. Terrified, there is no fleeing his demands. He repeatedly yells out our names until one of us goes into his bedroom.

"My back is hurting. Climb up here and massage my back."

He places a small vibrator in my hand and rolls over onto his stomach.

I gather up my long flannel nightie and crawl up onto his back. His warm, tanned skin presses against my legs, draped tightly against each side of him. I do as he instructs, pushing the tingling vibrator against his back.

"Lower—a little lower," he mumbles.

Sometimes, after only a few minutes, a deep, low rattling noise from his mouth tells me he has fallen asleep. Cautiously, with precise, slow movements, I crawl off him and tiptoe back to my room. Other times he rolls over onto his back, and the tickly vibrator is between us. As he presses the dancing vibrator against me, new and strange sensations overtake my private area and steal my breath. Then suddenly it is over, and the room becomes quiet. He isn't moving, and there is no more fast, heavy breathing. My nightgown and legs are sticky and wet, and I feel dirty. Imprinted into my young self is the rank smell of his breath, the sound of him groaning, the color and size of his arms, and the tingling feelings in my private parts. Pushing me away he rolls over, and I climb down from his bed.

I gather up the soiled pieces of me and the remnants of myself that evil could not steal and tremble as I make my way back to my room. I lie in bed, hating myself for going into his room and doing the things he told me to do. I feel shame, sick, and disgusted. I promise myself, next time I won't go; I just won't go. But fear of him overshadows my promises, and the next time he calls out my name I return to his room. Slowly, piece by piece, parts of me are dying.

The dawn always comes too quickly and signals it is time to get ready for school. I awaken in a fog. I haven't slept well. A heavy, sick feeling swirls in my stomach like I have done something bad, really bad.

I have a secret—a secret mixed with shame, confusion, fear, and even tinges of pleasure. Tired and confused, I tuck it away deep inside of me, certain no one would understand and wouldn't love me if they knew.

CHAPTER 13

Rear View

"Get in the car! Hurry! Hurry!"
Frantic, Mom tosses her purse into the car. Shaking uncontrollably, she uses both hands to insert the key into the ignition so we can flee the monster's rage. Unrelenting, he chases us and then clings to the car door as we drive off. As he yells and screams, his foot is pulled under the rear tire, crushing it. The foul words propelled toward us terrify me.

The humming of the tires on the asphalt road is a reassuring sound as the car moves further away. I turn and look through the rear window. Fear and relief commingle inside me as I see him flailing around on the ground. The vision of him becomes blurred as we move further and further away.

Driving away means distance from him. Driving away means safety. Simultaneously the rear-view image of him thrashing about on the pavement is etched into my mind.

* * *

There are happier times to look forward to, and the day has finally arrived: the getaway Christine and I have eagerly looked forward to for months.

Pushing my favorite stuffed animal, Honey Bear, into my suitcase, I zip it closed. Now I'm ready to go. Tomorrow Aunt Mill and Uncle Ozzie will come to pick us up. Every summer

Christine and I have gotten to spend a week with them in a paradise far removed from the world we know. It's a haven of fresh air, homegrown vegetables, fresh eggs collected from chicken coops, and frog hunting under long summer starlit nights. Magical, fun-filled, warm summer days come to an end, lulled to sleep by the soothing repetitive humming of irrigation systems and melodic chirping crickets.

It seems the minute we pile into their fancy car, our world changes. The soft leather seats smell rich and sweet, competing with Aunt Mill's abundance of musky Emeraude perfume. Instantly the familiar smells bring comfort. As I heard it, Aunt Mill and Uncle Ozzie were not able to have their own children. *No wonder they spoil us!* I think to myself. Dairy farmers, they have a farm in Livingston, California. Only a short seven miles from their house, Grandma and Grandpa Kluck have their house too. This makes it easy for them to come visit.

The trip is a four-and-a-half-hour drive full of laughter, singing, and storytelling. Uncle Ozzie tells stories about an enormous fish he caught and crazy chickens chasing Aunt Mill.

"Girls, wait till you see the surprise I have waiting for you!" Uncle Ozzie tells us. Christine and I giggle with excitement.

After hours of driving, traffic lights diminish, and we turn onto a dark, long road. I remember this road. This road is the last bit of the long journey. We are getting close, very close.

"Can I roll the window down, Aunt Mill?"

"Okay, but only for a minute or you'll be eating bugs," she responds with her low-pitched rolling laugh.

The window comes down, and I hang my head out, the dry wind blowing through my hair and into my face. Breathing in the aroma of the rich, fertile fields surrounding us, I look up, mesmerized by the dark night sky splattered with a zillion specks of sparkling light. Without notice a small bug is sucked into my nose and ends up in my throat.

"I swallowed a bug!" I spill out, coughing.

"I told you so!" Aunt Mill reminds me, and the car fills with laughter.

We unload the car and soon pile into bed in a neatly kept small bedroom. The exciting day has gotten the best of Christine and me. All we want to do is close our eyes and sleep. We have even forgotten about the big surprise Uncle Ozzie talked about.

Tuckered out, I breathe in the crisp, clean smell of cotton sheets and feel the softness of the blanket as I tuck them up under my chin. Aunt Mill plants her robust bottom on the edge of the bed, and together we close our eyes to pray a familiar nighttime prayer. While she prays I peek at her soft, round face and watch her mouth as the comforting words leave her lips.

"Now I lay me down to sleep; I pray the Lord my soul to keep. If I should die before I wake, I pray the Lord my soul He'll take."

Comfy and safe, soon we are fast asleep.

"Rise and shine!" Mr. Rooster declares well before sunrise.

Snuggling beneath warm blankets, with my arms wrapped around Honey Bear, I lie and listen to his morning territorial announcement.

Cock-a-doodle-do! he calls again and again.

Activity on the farm begins very early. Uncle Ozzie has already been up and at it, even before Mr. Rooster. Behind two large red barn doors are over twenty cows with udders full of milk. Milking is a big job and will take Uncle Ozzie several hours to finish. Once the milking is done, it's time for the cows' breakfast. Both Aunt Mill and Uncle Ozzie scurry about the barn to serve their black-and-white Holstein cows a mixture of corn silage and alfalfa hay. Uncle Ozzie wastes no time, heaving the hay mixture into bins for each hungry cow. While the contented cows chew away, he checks the water troughs, filling them with fresh water.

It's almost seven o'clock, and Christine and I mosey out of bed to get dressed. A wonderful aroma of sizzling bacon comes from the kitchen, where Aunt Mill is busy cooking breakfast.

I was told Aunt Mill graduated with a degree in Home Economics. The house is full of all her treasures. Her crochet doilies are beautifully placed on top of end tables, and her treasured ceramic figurine dolls are displayed throughout the house. A lovely lady in a green draped gown with a white, gold-trimmed bonnet catches my eye. They are all so delicately splendid and remind me of something I had forgotten. Mom and Aunt Mill used to paint ceramic dolls together when Daddy and Mom were still married. I remember carefully touching the delicate lace on Mom's ceramic dolls, always knowing they were her cherished treasures. "Be careful! These are not the kind of dolls you play with," she would caution me over and over as I sat and admired the intricate details, unable to resist a quick touch. Even so, I enjoyed hearing her tell stories about the many hours she and Aunt Mill spent together, making every beautiful detail.

Uncle Ozzie, dressed in faded jean overalls, bursts through the screen door in the kitchen.

"Well, were you two going to sleep all day?" he teases, winking at his wife.

"I'm hungry, Mildred, and something sure smells good!"

Gathered around the table, we are hungry and ready to dig into the sizzling, scrumptious food, but we wait as Aunt Mill blesses the food with a short prayer.

"This is so good, Aunt Mill!" we thank her.

We chatter, and soon Uncle Ozzie reminds us of the surprise he has. *That's right—a surprise!*

We remember and start gulping down our food in anticipation. Grabbing all the empty plates, we help Aunt Mill quickly wash and dry the dishes, eager to find out about our big surprise.

"Come on, kids!"

Uncle Ozzie motions for us to follow him. Aunt Mill hands him two good-sized bottles of warm milk, and out the door we go, trailing close behind him. We enter a small barn where several pens are lined with straw and contain two of the cutest baby calves. I can't ignore the overwhelming odor, but strangely I've come to like the smell of the barn—the familiar fragrance of manure, animals, feed, silage, and wood mixed together.

Uncle Ozzie hands us each a warm bottle full of milk.

"What do we do? How do we feed them?" we laugh, super excited and nervous.

Soon we are well on our way to nourishing the two adorable and hungry black-and-white spotted calves. As we hold the bottles upright, they tightly latch their mouths around the nipple, hurriedly sucking down the very last drop of warm milk.

Uncle Ozzie tells us, "These babies are yours, so you better come up with good names for them."

Molly comes to my mind, and Christine names hers Babe. During the week we get to feed them at least twice a day, brush them, and pet them. It doesn't take long before we become very attached to Molly and Babe. Without a doubt if sleeping in the barn were an option, we would spend the night curled up next to our soft, furry calves.

Taking part in the chores on the farm has a way of making me feel very important, proud, and part of the family. Gathering eggs from the chicken coop is Christine's job. One of the red-colored hens, Old Red, is feisty, and Aunt Mill tells stories about the hen chasing her when she collects the morning eggs. I'm relieved I wasn't given that job.

Aunt Mill takes great pride in her garden, and I'm given the job of keeping the weeds out and picking the vegetables for the day's supper. Aunt Mill had taught me how to carefully pull the bright-red tomatoes from the vines. I will never forget last summer when I met my first tomato worm, and I'm determined to avoid meeting one again. I grabbed the large, green, plump worm and smooshed it in my hand. I didn't mean to, but it looked so much like the vine it was climbing on that I didn't even see it. Shaking my hand, trying to flick off the creepy worm, I screamed all the way to the kitchen sink and turned the water on to wash it away. Aunt Mill had a big chuckle.

It's now midmorning, and Molly and Babe have devoured their warm milk. Rushing out the barn door, Uncle Ozzie greets the milk truck. They have come to load up the morning milk. Christine and I leave Molly and Babe and race to the top of a series of stacked bales of hay. From our vantage point, sitting on top of the hay, we can see far into the distance.

Simultaneously we feel big and small and free! So much open space! So different from the city life we are used to! Christine and I linger on top of the sweet, fresh-cut hay with the warmth of the sun hugging our faces. Oh, the joy and comfort of sitting so high where burdens vanish, and our world is safe.

The crunching sound of tires on gravel distracts us… then a loud car horn honks. Grandpa and Grandma Kluck pull into the horseshoe driveway in their green Ford Ranch Wagon. Christine, full of excitement, with me close behind her, climbs down the bales of hay as fast as she can to run and greet them.

Most days they make the short drive from Delhi to have lunch with Aunt Mill, their only daughter. The kitchen is once again full of mouthwatering smells. Aunt Mill's chicken salad sandwiches and homemade iced tea are ready. Christine exuberantly collides into Grandma's arms as Grandpa gives me a warm hug.

Grandpa's narrow, weathered face carries a huge smile as he shares stories about Daddy and Aunt Mill growing up. Harold was the oldest, and I guess he gave Aunt Mill a hard time. Grandpa has so many stories. His fishing stories are my favorite, even though I've heard them many times.

"We need to go to the canal," he says and promises to carve us one of his whistles out of sugar cane with his pocketknife.

After lunch he lets down the tailgate of his station wagon, and Christine and I climb onto it. Dangling our legs off the edge of the tailgate, we hang on for a fun, bumpy ride to the irrigation canals, giggling all the way. Grandpa does some fiddling with the irrigation equipment at the canal and then sits down in the shade with his back pressed against an old oak tree. He cuts a sugar cane in half with his pocketknife and begins to work his magic, whittling the cane into a whistle.

The day is warming up. Christine and I giggle, dipping our feet into the canal to cool off, as grasshoppers hop about us in short, low flights making muffled buzzing sounds. Occasionally Grandpa places the whistle to his lips to try it out, then his whittling continues, perfecting the whistles. We spend a little more than an hour at the canal. He makes one last adjustment to the equipment before we hop onto the tailgate of the station wagon and are ready for the excitement of the bumpy ride back.

Supper is served early on the farm, usually right before the last milking. Aunt Mill cleans up the kitchen one last time for the day, while Uncle Ozzie tends to the cows and washes down the milking barn. Right before bedtime we gather in the small living room, and Aunt Mill tells us about tomorrow's plans.

"We are going to drive to town, and I want you girls to pick out some fabric so I can make you some full-gathered skirts to take home with you." She also has another big surprise. "Vacation Bible School starts in the morning, right after chores. I've got you all signed up. So no dillydallying. We'll eat breakfast and scoot right out the front door."

Sleep comes easy at the farm. Our tummies are full, our bodies are a good weary from chores and playing, and there is nothing in the night we need to fear. Before we know it, the rooster is greeting us with his morning wake-up call. Breakfast is over, and dishes are washed and dried quickly. Back in my room, I plow through my suitcase, wondering just what to wear to Vacation Bible School.

These will look nice, I think to myself, retrieving peach-checkered shorts and a white sleeveless top with ruffles. My decision is made. Placing my foot on a chair, I buckle my white sandals and get a strong whiff of Aunt Mill's perfume. She is ready to go.

The Lutheran church is situated on a corner on Olive Street. As we park I see a lot of kids walking into the church.

"Come on now. You don't want to be late!" Three feet ahead of us, Aunt Mill urges us along.

My stomach feels uneasy. I don't know anyone except Christine. Immediately we are greeted by some older kids who introduce themselves. But instantly I forget their names. They help us find our classrooms, which are divided by age groups. Now my stomach is really churning. Christine and I are separated.

The room I'm in has a lot of kids who look my age. I make my way to an empty chair and sit down.

"Hi! My name is Kathy. What is your name?" the girl in the chair beside me says.

"My name is Kathy too!"

With great relief I smile. Certainly I won't forget her name! Soon all of us kids gather, sitting on the floor in a big circle. Helping me shed a little of my anxiety, Kathy sits right next to me.

Miss Sarah, our teacher, introduces herself while she hands each of us a piece of paper with words from the Bible written on it. Then she begins to read.

"For God so loved the world, He gave His only begotten Son, that whosoever believeth in Him should not perish, but have everlasting life."

Next Miss Sarah tells us a story from the Bible about a man named Moses being put into a basket and sent down a river.

After the story Kathy and I move to a table where we decorate a soup can with pretty, colored paper. We add some dirt to the can and plant a little flower. I can't wait to share my plant with Aunt Mill because she can plant a tiny seed, and it grows into a huge tomato plant.

After we are done with crafts, grape Kool-Aid and cookies are placed at our seats, and boy do they taste good. Miss Sarah asks us to form a long line, and we follow her to a huge room in the church. I see an enormous cross in the front of the room. Sunlight is shining through beautiful colored stained-glass windows right behind the cross. The room is filled with the other kids, who are all singing, "Jesus loves me! This I know, for the Bible tells me so. Little ones to Him belong. They are weak, but He is strong. Yes, Jesus loves me! Yes, Jesus loves me! Yes, Jesus loves me! The Bible tells me so!" I look around for Christine, but there are too many kids to find her. Kathy and I join the rest of our class and the other kids in singing.

It has been a great day. I made new friends, Kathy, Betty, Debbie, and Miss Sarah, my teacher. I can't wait to come back tomorrow. Everyone is so nice. I feel really happy and special. Jesus loves *me*!

* * *

It has been the best week of my life on Aunt Mill and Uncle Ozzie's dairy farm. Today, the last day of Vacation Bible School, all of us kids will put on a little play for our families. I'm excited! Aunt Mill, Uncle Ozzie, Grandpa, and Grandma Kluck will be here.

All the families arrive and gather in the big room with the big cross. We sing songs together, and our play is a big hit. Finally each of us receives a Vacation Bible School completion certificate with our name printed on it. Pride swells inside me as I run my finger over my name on the piece of paper.

Outside, an oak tree shades a large grassy area. Several picnic tables are covered with colorful plastic tablecloths where we share special treats, like one big family.

Eventually we exchange hugs and say goodbye to our new friends. It's bittersweet after such a fun week together. But tomorrow Christine and I go home and take a lot of special memories with us. *Maybe next summer we will see them again,* I think to myself as I look out the rear window of Aunt Mill's car. I wave goodbye to my new friends, the white church with the big cross, and the beautiful stained-glass windows.

Today is our last day on the farm for this summer's visit. Tomorrow we head home. Aunt Mill is busy doing our laundry and hemming the beautiful full skirts she made us. Outside in the small barn, Christine is spending every minute she can with her calf, Babe. As usual Uncle Ozzie is tending to his chores. In the small bedroom, Grandma Kluck and I are cuddled together. She loves to take naps, and I like being close to her. If I could I would stay here, snuggled up to her, and never go home. Gently she wraps a strand of my curly hair around one of her fingers over and over. My eyes are getting sleepy.

"I wish I could take Molly home with me," I quietly say to her, already knowing it is impossible. Her soft touch soothes, and I feel sleepier and sleepier. But then Grandma leans close to my ear and whispers.

"You know, Harold is not your father. He is not your daddy."

I'm startled and confused. As I'm nuzzled up next to her, motionless, her words echo through my thoughts. Harold is not my daddy? What does that mean? A heavy sadness sweeps over me, and sleep is the furthest thing from my mind.

Mr. Rooster says good morning to us like he does every day. Does he know how much I'll miss his morning greetings? Uncle Ozzie loads our suitcases into the trunk of his car. Running to the barn, Christine and I want to hug Molly and Babe and say goodbye. We wrap our arms around their warm, soft necks and hold them tight for as long as we can.

"Come on girls, come on," we hear Uncle Ozzie call out to us. "Grandpa and Grandma Kluck have come to say goodbye."

Pressing into Grandpa's chest, I soak in his warm hug and the unique menthol smells from his pain ointments. I don't want to let go. With a sweet grin covering his face, he pulls a special whittled whistle out of his pocket and places it in my hand.

Grandma Kluck is hugging Christine. Feeling uneasy after what she said to me, I would like to step around her, but I can't. I leave Grandpa's embrace, give Grandma a quick hug, and climb into the car. Immediately I turn around, looking out the rear window, cherishing my last glimpses of the farm—the sanctuary where so many memories have been created.

Feeling sad I silently say my goodbyes. *Goodbye to the big red barn where all the cows are milked, to the huge stack of hay bales we climbed where we felt big and safe. Goodbye to all the chickens freely strutting about, to Molly and Babe, and to the scrumptious smells cooked from Aunt Mill's beautiful garden.*

Through the window I see Grandma Kluck waving goodbye. Her eyes meet mine. I don't want to think about the words she whispered in my ear, but I can't help it. As we drive off, she gets farther and farther away until I can barely see her. I turn around and settle in for the long drive to Long Beach.

Out the window the beautiful sanctuary passes by: miles and miles of alfalfa fields, pastures sheltering Holstein cows and their babies, and irrigation systems humming. I roll down the window, breathing in the sweet smell of fresh-cut hay. Longingly I look back at the road behind us. Sadness mingled with joy settles in while the street vibrates underneath, and we drive further and further away. The rear-view images are forever etched in my heart.

Sanctuary

A world of wonder, bright and new
Where starry skies shine on cue
Filling children's curious minds
With dreams and wonder so sublime

In morning glow, the rooster crows
RISE AND SHINE, and off he goes
And so, they waved goodbye the night
to see God's kiss of morning light

Like a flower drawing from the earth,
the children drink it in…
Winds that blow through limbs of wheat,
Whistles whittled oh so sweet
Climbing hay bales which tickle feet
Collecting eggs from Momma hens
Feeding calves till warm milk ends

Free from burdens, free to play
Oh, how the children wish they could stay
Where safe and sound and people pray…
Jesus Loves Me on this day

CHAPTER 14

Learning the Delicate Dance

The sun has long set, and the house is full of scrumptious smells. Christine and I have a little homework to finish up. My sixth-grade teacher, Mrs. Struck, is expecting my final report on Nathan Hale tomorrow. Christine's eighth-grade classes seem much harder than mine. She has a huge math test coming up she has been studying for. However, our girl chatter and the delicious aromas wafting out from the kitchen momentarily push homework out of our thoughts. In a world of her own, Janice just ended a phone call with her high school sweetheart, Ronnie, and is finishing setting the table for supper. She is excited because they have a date right after dinner.

It smells delicious. Clanking spoons against pans, Mom transfers the hot meal onto serving dishes: fried pork chops, boiled potatoes, corn, and a tossed green salad. Don has already taken his chair and made himself comfortable at the table. Uneasily I squeeze around him without touching him or looking at him. Taking our usual seats, we sit quietly and wait for Mom to join us.

We've learned to be silent while weighing and measuring the dinnertime atmosphere. Tonight it is unavoidable. The smell of alcohol is oozing out of him. Have they both been drinking? Janice, Christine, and I cautiously exchange glances. I can see it in their eyes…they notice it too.

Don dishes up a portion of salad for himself. A small plate of saltine crackers is a requirement if salad is part of the meal. I will never forget the time Mom forgot to put them on the table, and all hell broke loose. Now, smearing butter over one of the saltines, he begins eating.

No one is talking. Every clink and clatter of the passing serving dishes resonates around the table. With his salad gone, he cuts into a pork chop and scoops up a bite of potato. The silence is broken.

"Blanche, get your fucking coat!" he commands.

"Why do I need my coat?" Mom calmly and quietly responds.

"Get your goddamn coat and get your ass to the store. You must need salt because it's all in these damn potatoes!"

Mom's voice rises. "I'm not going to the store. We have plenty of salt in the cupboard!"

With my fork I push my food around on my plate as fear wells up inside me, and I begin shaking. I look at my sisters and see the unease on their faces. No one is eating.

Don pushes his plate off to the side. The muscles in his face are taut with rage. Abruptly he stands up, the serving dish of potatoes in hand, and heaves the plate against the kitchen wall. In a rage he picks up the platter of pork chops and throws it across the kitchen. Then Mom's silence breaks too. The shouting between them fills the room.

Mom steps a few feet from the table, ready to walk away and be done with the argument. But a tight grip on the back of her hair halts her movement.

"Where do you think you're going?"

There's loud screaming—cursing—crying—everything is happening at once. Christine can't take one more minute of it.

She jumps up yelling, "Leave her alone! Leave her alone!"

Don swings at Mom, his fist planting in the center of her face. She falls to the floor with blood dripping from her nose. Teeth clenched, Christine lunges at him, pounding on his back.

Oblivious to Christine, he mumbles, "All the goddamn salt is in the fucking potatoes!"

Stumbling from the kitchen, he makes his way to the bedroom, leaving us to pick up the mess. Tears mix with the blood on Mom's face. Janice kneels down beside her, carefully blotting the blood with a napkin. Trembling, Christine and I stand back against the wall. It isn't long before Ronnie arrives to pick up Janice for their date.

We've picked up most of the food in the kitchen and moved to the living room. We huddle next to Mom on the sofa, knowing exactly what to do. We've had lots of practice. We don't turn on any lights, run water, or flush the toilet. We sit in silence, fearful of awakening the drunken giant. We stare into the dark, and the minutes go by—burdened, heavy, unending. Face to face, even in the darkness, I can see Mom's hand pressed against her mouth and nose where he hit her.

I feel panic stir, but I won't let it out. I tremble and pray he has fallen asleep. It feels like we've been sitting for hours when the worst possible thing happens. We hear him. Suddenly light from the hallway breaks the darkness that has been hiding us. From the sofa we can see him, bent over, stooped inside the hallway linen closet, muttering and fumbling around. Christine and I know what he is doing. He is looking through the peephole in the linen closet.

Terrified, I close my eyes tightly. Despite my every effort to be frozen, a couple of tears slowly roll down my cheeks, threatening to unleash all the fear welled up inside me. *See, Mom, we were telling the truth about him!* I assert silently to myself. Recognizing my growing distress, Mom gently places her hand over my mouth. I must be silent. I must be still. I must not make a sound.

Tonight we are lucky. In his drunken stupor, he backs out of the closet and stumbles back to his bedroom. We hear the door shut behind him. Hopefully it's over for tonight. Hopefully the lessons we've learned have been enough, at least for tonight.

CHAPTER 15

Click

I reach over and push down the button. One *click* and the piercing sound of my alarm ceases. My body isn't ready to get out of bed.

After the horrible dinner, the night had been fleeting and restless. Puffy eyed from lack of sleep, I drag around the heavy, sick feeling in my stomach while I get ready for school. I think about the homework I should have done and hope Mrs. Struck will give me one more day to turn it in. I bet she will. She has always been so nice to me, giving me near perfect grades for my cursive writing and reading. Why didn't I do my homework? I hate disappointing her and will probably be the only one in my class who didn't do it. On top of not doing my homework, I'm late. My friends have already left for school. Even so, today I welcome walking to school alone.

As I get closer to school, anxiety stirs so I push myself to walk a little faster. Finally I make it to the front entrance of Cubberley Elementary. Quiet and empty playgrounds confirm how late I am. Still I can't ignore the pressure in my tummy. I have to stop at the bathroom before heading to Mrs. Struck's sixth-grade classroom. Maybe going to the bathroom will help me feel better. I push open the heavy metal door and find an empty stall. *Click.* I lock the door behind me. As I sit down to go potty, I look down at my dangling feet. Inside my white tennis shoes, my bobby socks have managed to slip under the heels of my feet. While tugging on my socks, I notice someone's shoes in the stall next to me. All done, I adjust my clothes and come out of the stall. Kelly, my neighborhood girlfriend, comes out of the stall next to me.

"You're late!" she informs me as if I didn't already know. "What the heck is that?" she points down toward my knees.

I look down and see my long pink floral nightgown protruding below my dress. I feel my cheeks get hot. I don't know what to say to her.

"It's my nightgown. I guess I forgot to take it off," I respond, feeling stupid.

In my murky state this morning, I had put my dress on right over my nightgown. Kelly shakes her head, laughing. Together we pull up my nightgown, tucking it into my panties, making my dress puff out in all the wrong places. I join her laughter, but inside I cringe, wondering how I could be so stupid.

The day goes by quickly. Mrs. Struck nicely allows me to bring my overdue homework in tomorrow, but not one day later. I smile at her and think about how much I like her. She has a way about her that makes me want to do my very best. I make a promise to myself: I will do my homework as soon as I get home.

After school I quickly make my way home. As I reach the corner of Shadypark and Carfax, I can see our house and Don's truck parked in the driveway. *Why is he home so early?* I wonder, and my stomach drops. Mom's car is not there. I walk slower and slower, trying to prolong reaching the front door. I could hop the fence and go to Charlotte's. No, I really need to do my homework. I can't let Mrs. Struck down again.

It is a beautiful sunny day, and I can see the front door is open, allowing the warmth to escape through the screen. I gather myself as I step forward. I open the screen door and hear Don talking loudly to Christine—something about school, I think. Christine is in eighth grade at Marshall Junior High School…the school I will be going to next year. Maybe Don is yelling at her for pounding on his back last night. Christine is bravely yelling back at him. I set my schoolwork down in our bedroom, remove my dress and nightgown, and find something comfy to put on. I sit on my bed for a few minutes until I notice their loud interaction has stopped. Almost too afraid to look, but failing to block my own curiosity, I creep back out of our room.

Two of the kitchen chairs are in front of the mirror in the living room. With exaggerated movements, Don is waving something in his hand, motioning for us to come sit. What is he doing? Confused, I timidly sit on one of the chairs facing the mirror. Even Christine is silent now. Following his orders, she sits next to me on the other chair. Looking into the mirror, I see it!

Is that a gun? Yes, he has a gun in his hand! What is he doing with a gun? He spins a part of the gun repeatedly, and I can't help but think this is a dream. It couldn't possibly get any worse…and it has. I don't move, not even a finger. I know how angry he gets. *Kathy, don't move, don't move…*I tell myself. I am so terrified I can barely breathe. *Am I going to die?*

"One bullet!" he says to us. He spins it again and again. "*Sit. Just sit here!*" His voice is loud and angry.

We are frozen. I watch his every move in the mirror. Occasionally he looks away from us, over to the screen door.

I feel screams welling up in my throat, but I force myself to be silent.

I want to grab my sister's hand, but I'm paralyzed by the sheer terror pounding through me. I dare not move.

Then I hear Mom's car pull into our driveway. Thank God. Mom is home! She'll stop him. Mom won't let him go on!

Don places the gun on the side of Christine's head. I watch in horror as the cold metal reflects the light shining in through the windows—the shining cold metal now pressed to *my sister's* head. Powerless, I look into the mirror and see her eyes scrunched closed with big tears streaming down her face.

Click!

Moments later he places the cold end of the gun to my head. *Wait—stop!* I want to scream.

Click!

There is no bullet. No loud explosion of noise like what I expected. Just that cold metallic *click* that resonates through my trembling body.

He brings the gun back to Christine's head, then that *click* resounds…and then it is my turn again. Back and forth, back and forth.

Mom, who has finally made her way to the house, stands on the other side of the screen door and unleashes a throat-wrenching scream, dropping her purse on the porch. She moves, waves her hands, and pleads with Don to stop. But he doesn't listen. He pulls the trigger.

Click!

"*Please, please, stop!*" Mom's voice is guttural with uninhibited panic.

He pulls the trigger again.

Click!

Suddenly Mom's screams stop. I can't hear her. Is she gone? Did she leave us? That thought—leaving us alone with this man holding a gun to our heads—is too much.

Please, Mom, please don't leave us! I scream as loud as I possibly can…but my lips don't move. I cried out for my mother, but only in my head. I don't dare turn to look for her. Don walks over to the screen door.

"Blanche! Blanche! Bitch!" he screams.

"Don, please stop this! Please!" I hear her voice in the distance. Don returns and places the gun to Christine's head. The terror continues.

To me it feels like it lasts for hours, but I don't know how long the terror continued. At some point the police show up. They are outside our house, and after some time and negotiating, they coax Don out onto the front porch. Swiftly a different kind of *click* resounds, and the police officers handcuff him. They take him away.

Police gather around Christine and me.

"You are going to be fine. He is gone," a nice woman softly speaks to us.

I want to cry, but I have no tears. I want to be thankful, but my limbs won't stop shaking. I feel dazed and numb, watching everyone talking and busy around us. Mom is over in a corner, sobbing. I hear someone say Janice is on her way. It feels like everyone is moving around the room in slow motion.

A few days later, we pack up our belongings and move to a two-bedroom apartment fifteen minutes away. The school year is ending, so Mom will drive us to school for the remaining few days. It will be a relief to not have to go to school, I think.

Every day, anxiety overwhelms me. Simple things like reading are not easy. I can't concentrate or focus. I have nightmares about someone chasing me. I'm running as fast as I can but going nowhere. The dream doesn't end until I startle awake, terrified, my heart racing. Sometimes I find myself staring off into space as *click...click...click...* echoes through my head.

But Don is gone now. Janice told me he is gone. She told me he was sent to some sort of prison.

Click! He is locked up behind bars!

Am I safe now?

CHAPTER 16

Saving Graces

During those years with Don, I dreaded nights, not knowing what was going to happen. But sometimes when Don was gone fishing or moved out because of a horrible fight, there were good nights—even magical nights when a special light broke through and overshadowed the darkness. Albert Schweitzer once said, "There are two means of refuge from the miseries of life: music and cats." Very early on in my life, this was true for me.

There are certain possessions in one's home that one cannot live without, or the absence of that particular item could sorely impact the song of one's life. For me it was a phonograph! Five feet long and sleekly embodied in mahogany, the Magnavox console rested against a wood-paneled wall in our small living room. The heart of this piece of furniture, the phonograph, provided an escape. I could nestle up to one of the mesh-covered speakers and soak in the warmth of every vibration. I could spend hours lost in a different world because music opened my heart and pierced through the numbness I had cocooned myself in. I had favorite songs I would play over and over, losing myself in every word pulsating through the speakers.

Often my sister Janice would carefully stack her favorite forty-fives, activate the turntable, and adjust the volume loudly enough for our nearest neighbors to hear. With endless layers of petticoats twirling, she and my sister Christine would spend hours dancing to Elvis, Jerry Lee Lewis, and the Big Bopper. Tall, slender, and blessed with long, chestnut-brown hair, Janice performed all the latest moves with ease, and Christine quickly caught on. Mostly I was content to curl up on the worn, pink sectional tucked in the corner of our small living room. I would absorb the resounding vibrations of the phonograph while passively waiting for an invitation to join them. Occasionally the mood would turn somber as the recording of "Old Shep" gently slipped down from the stack, landing beneath the needle, and Elvis would softly croon about his beloved dog Shep and his death. The simple yet poignant words to this song stirred a longing in my young heart for someone to love me that much.

A new song would drop beneath the needle, and then another. For hours this was the routine. I cherished the moments when I briefly felt included in their tightly woven sisterhood oasis. The music, movements, and joy united us and filled our small living room with laughter, ripping off the bondages of fear, if only for a short time.

In my early teens, when my heart was first secretly tickled by the exhilarating arrow of fictitious love, I vividly remember snuggling up close to the console, resting my head against the pulsating speaker, and submerging myself into the love song, "Angel Baby," by Rosie and the Originals. Before long I was whisked away into an imaginary romance with Danny Webster, the most popular seventh-grade boy at Marshall Junior High. I would savor that moment until the last notes played and the repetitious sound of the needle, stuck at the end of the record, interrupted my innocent pleasure.

Like a cherished friend, the phonograph frequently provided me sweet interludes of escape and temporarily silenced the violence that often occupied our home. Not once did the phonograph disappoint me. Whether through the Temptations, the Supremes, or Johnny Mathis, it was always available to speak lyrics that would soothe my soul and transport my mind on a journey of dancing above the tragic conditions around me.

There was another source of happiness in our lives. At one point in time, seventeen was the count, if counting was even possible. There were orange ones, tabbies, a calico, a black-and-white one, and all varying ages.

It all started in the summer of 1961 with Buttercup, my first sweet calico kitten. After surviving a horrifying gun experience, Mom moved us from our house into a small two-bedroom apartment. It wasn't long before my beautiful sisters, Janice and Christine, made friends with a couple of single guys. Gene and Spider lived downstairs from us in apartment number twenty-six. My sisters would disappear for hours and come home chattering and laughing among themselves about their new handsome friends. It seemed both of them were smitten with Spider, a tall, lanky, free-spirited type. I would overhear some of the details of the two of them plotting their next exciting rendezvous. My loneliness intensified during this time. After all, why would they want me tagging along?

The days seemed long and lonely. I would peer out the bedroom window, where in the distance I could see Carson Street. Anxiously I would look for Mom's car among the traffic, hoping she would be home soon.

Buttercup and babies

One day I saw a sign pushed into the lawn in front of a small house next door to the apartments. "FREE KITTENS," it read. Curious, I walked the short distance to take a look. Curled up among her five brothers and sisters, her unique little face stood out, capturing my attention. Her mixture of orange, black, and gray fur included a little black smudge near the tip of her nose. When I picked her up and held her against my chest, she started to softly purr, and I knew I had to have her. Although she was free, I insisted on paying twenty-five cents for her. Twenty-five cents would surely guarantee my ownership. No one could take her from me.

Buttercup helped see me through that summer. I would cuddle with my new furry companion for hours. She became my little shadow who reminded me I wasn't alone. If I went to the bathroom without her, she would squeeze her paw under the door as if to wave at me, conveying, "Hey, you left me out here!" She would lie beside me, purring her little heart out. At night Buttercup curled around my head and often kneaded my hair with her little paws. We moved back home at the end of summer, and Buttercup went with us.

While one or two cats are optimum, Buttercup was only the beginning. I began bringing cats home I was convinced had been abandoned. Most of these fur babies likely already had a home, but this became a means of putting a Band-Aid over my pain. I discovered a love and acceptance flowing from my furry felines, and adding one more could only ensure this love would never go away. I also believed the lost or abandoned cat was yearning for love like I was. I was absolutely certain they welcomed my rescue.

When three of our cats became pregnant at the same time, we ended up with little kitties playing and scurrying about everywhere. Kitty litter boxes couldn't contain or eliminate the odor that pervaded our house. It was becoming evident taking care of so many cats properly had its challenges.

I didn't see it that way, but Mom did. One day she came home from work with a large gunnysack and a package of bologna. She began collecting the cats and was on a mission to take them to the humane society, hopefully to be rehomed.

It was devastating to watch her gather them up and eventually drive off. I sat on the sofa, dumping buckets of tears. When I ran out of tears, I sat in silence looking around the empty living room. Scared and hunkered down under an end table was one orange cat who had managed to escape Mom's gunnysack. Magically a gray tabby also peered out from under the sofa. They were frightened. However, with a little coaxing and lots of petting, they began to purr. I gathered up the two remaining fur babies and retreated to my bedroom. Later that day, although frustrated she had missed two, Mom agreed to let me keep them.

My cats were angels with fur. They introduced me to unconditional love, loyalty, and a lot of comfort amid the chaos surrounding me. While my four-legged furry felines helped me survive day to day, music had the amazing power to transport me above the chaos, creating magical times of joy, laughter, and freedom. Maya Angelou stated it well: "Music was my refuge. I could crawl into the spaces between the notes and curl my back to loneliness." My furry friends and music were incredible gifts, "saving graces" that helped me survive.

CHAPTER 17

Betrayal

The perspiration dripping into my eyes stings, making it difficult to see. Still I keep running. My heart pounding, I run as fast as I can. It's over eighty degrees, and the heavy coat that has become my daily uniform weighs me down as sweat pours down my face. My coat has become my protective shield, an attempt to hide the constant perspiration and unpleasant odor that plague me. Shimmering trees and house after house are in my peripheral vision, moving in slow motion while Mr. Whalen's words do loops through my mind: "Is there something going on at home?"

Home! Mom inserts the key into the doorknob as Christine and I stand behind her on the front porch—the same porch where she had stood pleading with Don to stop his horrendous act of violence.

Mom turns the key and pushes the door open. The house has been closed up for months. Cold and musty, it smells like all the fresh air has been sucked out. Stepping inside, I see that everything looks the same. But it isn't the same.

Slowly I meander through each room. The furniture is positioned just like we left it. On top of the piano in my bedroom, my treasured collection of small ceramic animals sits, just as I left it, only now laden with dust. I look into my closet, where shoes and clothes remain strewn on the floor, just like I left them.

An invisible veil separates me from the things I once cared about. Pieces of Don are here and there; the two chairs still sit in front of the mirror he placed us in front of, the peephole in the hall closet still there, and the bedroom he summoned us to. Nothing seems to have changed much, except for Christine and me. There are parts of us that will never be the same and parts of us that died.

Janice doesn't move back in with us. She had surprised everyone, running off to Las Vegas and marrying her high school sweetheart, Ronnie. Although the house now belongs to Mom, Christine, and me, and of course Buttercup, Don has left an indelible mark.

As summer ends, I nervously anticipate seventh grade, my first year at Marshall Junior High School. Marshall Junior High School is definitely a change from Cubberley Elementary. There are a lot of new things to learn. I now have numerous classes and have to figure out where they are and how to get to them on time. I have my own locker where I keep all the books I've been given, and there are a lot of them. On top of that, every class has a different teacher, not just one, like I'm used to. After my first week, I have a list of supplies I will need to ask Mom to get for me. Already it seems I will have a lot more homework than I did at Cubberley.

At Marshall Junior High, I pour all of my energy into getting good grades. My teachers' positive comments feed my hungry spirit. Pleasing them becomes my mission and the payoff of positive praises my anchor.

I have big shoes to fill at Marshall Junior High. Christine, finishing up her last year as a ninth grader, is popular. She has set several records in track, and I am determined to try and break them.

My sister is a beautiful girl, with long chestnut hair and a spark in her big brown eyes. It is apparent to me that boys at school gravitate to her beauty and personality. Secretly I struggle with the social changes that seem to come so easily for others. I see girls walking with boys, holding hands, putting their arms around each other, and even kissing. Curious, I take it all in, terrified at the thought of any boy making a movement toward touching me.

Seventh grade goes by so fast! I excel even with all the new challenges of middle school and adjustments at home. My report card beams with all A's and a lot of encouraging comments from my teachers. "Kathy is very pleasant and cooperative. She is a pleasure to have in my class." I read and reread their words, letting them soak in like a thirsty, dry sponge. Inside I beam and think, *Maybe I am smart.*

Things at home are different with Don gone. I finally find I can sleep without worrying about his drunken intrusions. With Janice now married, Christine and I have the house to ourselves. Mom is almost always gone, usually at work, which leaves us a lot of unsupervised freedom. Occasionally she gets home very late into the evening, stopping after work for a few beers.

Our house has a flow of friends coming and going. There had been a time when for unspoken reasons our friends were forbidden to come to our house, and now with Don gone, friends visit on a regular basis. It feels good to know they like hanging out at our house and their parents approve.

Now Christine and I crank up the phonograph and dance together. I enjoy dancing with her, and when Mom comes home from a long day at work, we have her to ourselves. We help her count her tips, and Christine will spruce up her French roll hairdo, ratting her fine hair and spraying it firmly in place.

One day Mom comes home with a tetherball for us. Lacking all the appropriate tools, but not lacking determination, she digs out a hole in the middle of our driveway with a hammer, a screwdriver, and of course a can of Coors beer. The tetherball pole never stands completely upright, but it doesn't matter. We spend hours hitting the ball around a pole that lists to the right or left, depending on which way the ball is sent soaring.

With Don gone my unease and tension slowly seem to dissipate, and laughter comes more freely. At the end of summer, I look forward to eighth grade. For the first time, I will be at school without my older sister.

September arrives before I know it, and so does eighth grade and a whole set of new teachers. I like all my teachers, but it doesn't take me long to decide Mr. Whalen, my English teacher, is my favorite. After only a few weeks of class, I feel at ease around him. Mr. Whalen is quick witted, and his sense of humor mingles with tremendous kindness.

"How are you today, Miss Kathy?" I can count on him asking me with a pinch of an accent. I like hearing him say my name, and in secret I wonder if I might be his favorite student.

It's March, seven months into the school year. This morning I sit at my desk in Mr. Whalen's classroom. I pull my coat tightly around me to hide my perspiration. I tilt my head toward my arm and breathe to see if my perspiration is creating a dreaded odor. I sit and wait for class to start.

Chatter fills the classroom as other students file in and take their seats. Mr. Whalen's class is right before lunch, and already it is warm. I hear the bell ring, indicating we should all be in our seats ready to start class. The chatter lessens, and I see Mr. Whalen walking toward my desk. He gently touches my shoulder.

"Could I talk with you out in the hallway?"

The classroom turns silent as I get up from my desk and follow Mr. Whalen out into the hall.

The hallway is empty…just Mr. Whalen and me and a hallway lined with metal lockers. Clenching my coat tightly, I try to make eye contact with him, but it's hard. Something is different about Mr. Whalen. He looks so serious.

"Kathy, are you okay? I am very concerned about you. Your schoolwork has changed dramatically, and you just don't seem focused or yourself lately."

My heart is pounding, and I'm sweating like I'm in a sauna. I don't know what to say to him. I don't say anything. I see a little glimmer of light reflecting off the glass doors at the end of the hall. Momentarily I feel like I'm in a tunnel all by myself. As he continues, his words sound muffled and slow.

"Is everything okay at home?"

My heart is pounding in my ears. I have no words. I look at the doors at the end of the hall, and before I realize it, I'm running toward them as fast as I can. I push the doors open and keep running and running and running. I want to get home.

* * *

Home! A month earlier, Mom didn't come home. She didn't come home from work on Friday, and we didn't hear from her on Saturday. By Sunday Christine and I were frantic with worry.

We called Janice. Janice came over, and as we sat together, she called nearby hospitals to see if Mom had gotten in an accident or something.

Then the phone rang. Janice went to the kitchen, where the phone hung on the wall. She picked it up. Christine and I sat silently and listened.

"Mom! Where are you? You've been drinking! We've been worried sick about you! How could you do this? How could you?" Janice slammed the phone down.

"She did it! She married Don again!" Janice blurted out furiously.

Stunned, I sat numbly, processing Janice's words as numerous questions swirled through my mind. *Mom, how could you do this? Is this for real? Don is coming back…What will happen to us?* Only a few feet away is the mirror—the mirror he placed us in front of, and then a blaring *click* resonates through my mind. I place my hands over my ears to stop the sound.

Christine, fuming, began to yell.

"No! No!"

Later that day Christine's boyfriend, Bill, came to our house. Christine, filled with anger, haphazardly shoved her clothes into brown paper grocery bags, and Bill carried them out to his car. Spewing her anger, Christine got into his car, and I watched as the two of them drove away.

The next day was daunting. I felt dazed, afraid, hopeless, and confused. School was often the one place where I received a little encouragement from my teachers, but today I could barely function.

When I got home from school, Don and Mom were at the house. I went inside and anxiously sat down on the sofa. My insides held a mixture of feelings: anger, fear, and disbelief. I couldn't bear the thought of looking at him, let alone being near him again. *I wish Christine was here. She would let Mom have it! She would really let her know how horrible and wrong this is.*

The conversation with Mom was brief. She assured me everything would be okay, and things would be different.

"Plus, if he ever lays a hand on me, just call the police," she told me.

A few minutes later, she headed out the door to go to the grocery store.

For the first time since he held a gun to my head, I was alone with Don. I walked into the kitchen to get away from him, but I could feel him close behind me. I could smell him. The kitchen was painfully small for the two of us. It had been a long time since I'd smelled his presence and heard his breathing.

I watched him walk over and pick up my fishbowl. *Now what?* I wondered, as my insides tightened. He opened the door out to the backyard and dropped the bowl on the driveway. The glass bowl shattered. Water splashed everywhere. My small, orange goldfish flopped about among the broken shards of glass. Horrified and stunned, I stood frozen. A cold terror pounded inside me as I watched this evil man twist and turn his foot on my helpless, tiny fish until it stopped moving.

No words were exchanged. I fell mute. Within minutes Don made his point terrifyingly clear. Nothing had changed.

Mom returned home from the grocery store after a while, and I didn't say a word about what had happened. I didn't dare. I retreated to my bedroom and coiled up in my bed. I wanted to pound my fists on his face and scream, but I had no voice. I wanted to cry, but I had no tears. As I clenched my eyes, invisible walls rose up around me. Fear, shame, and uncertainty knocked, but finally sleep came and wouldn't let them in.

* * *

School, a safe place where I once thrived, is now painfully difficult. I can't focus or concentrate. Still I try because I don't want to let my teachers down. I want them to like me, think well of me, and I need their praises. Weighed down with un-bearable emotional chaos, I hide my nervous sweating under-neath my coat, hoping no one will notice that something is wrong.

But they do notice. Today Mr. Whalen noticed.

Exhausted and hot from running, I'm finally home. I go directly to my bedroom and shut the door behind me. I peel off my sweat-drenched coat and climb into bed, pulling the blankets up over my head. Mr. Whalen's words reverberate through my mind.

"Your schoolwork has changed dramatically…Is some-thing going on at home?"

I have really let him down. I know I have. I curl up and wait for sleep to bring me relief. Slowly I move into a men-tal space of emptiness, detached, where peace finally comes—where everything is silent, still, and no one can touch me.

How Can I?

How can I tell you what I don't understand?
How can I tell you I need your helping hand?
How can I tell you about secrets hidden deep?
How can I tell you my only refuge is found in sleep?

How can I tell you what your kindness means?
How can I tell you when only my inner voice has wings?
How can I let you down when you believe in me?
All I want is to please you and for you to see me free!

How can I tell you there is no place I belong?
How can I tell you of things so very wrong?
How can I tell you of parts of me let go?
How can I tell you what I don't even know?

How can I tell you what I don't even know?
HOW?
HOW CAN I?

CHAPTER 18

Cocoon

I am embarrassed to see Mr. Whalen the next day. I wonder what he will say to me. It isn't just Mr. Whalen. I don't feel comfortable anywhere. Shut down, withdrawn, I watch as my classmates chat among themselves. I take it all in…conversations about their newest crushes, the slumber party they are looking forward to, what they brought for lunch, what they had for dinner, homework, and so on. It doesn't matter what the conversations are about, I stand on the outside looking in. I have nothing to add.

I don't think anyone notices the demons I carry. The other side of my pain is a façade of nodding my head yes and mastered smiles in an effort to fit in and hide what I do not understand. Constrained, locked inside my own world, there is nowhere I feel comfortable, except when sleep gives me respites of peace.

Life at home has not changed except for one thing. I am alone with Don. Christine continues to live with her boyfriend. Mom and I visit Christine a couple of times. We take her some groceries; however, Christine's anger toward Mom overshadows any gratitude for the token gesture. Our visits are brief. Christine seems different to me. The spark in her beautiful brown eyes has morphed into anger. She looks older and acts older, like she has become a grown-up overnight. But she doesn't look happy. She has entered into a different kind of survival mode, one where she tries to let go of the horrible world she left and take care of herself.

Don, still volatile and unpredictable, explodes in a rage one afternoon. He is completely out of control. He drags Mom out onto the driveway, hitting her as she screams for him to stop. Remembering Mom's words, I reach for the phone on the kitchen wall. Don immediately leaves Mom on the driveway, grabs me, and hurls me across the kitchen, slamming me into the kitchen cabinets. He turns and yanks the phone off the wall. Beat up and distraught, Mom sits up on the driveway in tears. With the wind knocked out of me, I lie sprawled on the kitchen floor. I look around, and Don is gone. Then I hear his truck screech away, and I am able to breathe a sigh of relief.

Don moves out of the house on Carfax to an apartment about thirty minutes from us in Downey. Shortly after, Mom begins spending weekends with Don. On Friday she leaves me a green roll of dimes equaling five dollars. It is to buy myself food or anything I need for the weekend. She returns Sunday afternoon or evening. I am relieved he is gone. I hope he will never come back. I also know there are no guarantees.

I internalize the loneliness, fear, and anger I feel, moving into a space where feelings are blocked, and I dissociate from emotions. I no longer have tears, no longer feel anger, no longer feel. I know I am somehow deeply different from others, but I don't know why.

I am loosely tethered to fragile lifelines: a few teachers, a few friends, and my fur babies. I can't share what I don't understand. I don't understand enemies who don't materialize into anything I know how to battle. The unbearable weight of depression collapses inward as I wonder, *Why am I so different?* Shame pins me down in paralyzing darkness and emotional exile as I torment myself for participating in his evil acts, not standing up to him, and failing in school. Fear leaves an imprint I carry with every breath I take, and helplessness snuffs out hope. Intertwined together, the burden of these overwhelming feelings is too great to bear.

So I spin myself a protective cocoon: sleep. Sleep becomes a deeply rooted reflex. Any time I feel danger, or the slightest bit uncomfortable, sleep is my refuge and the only way I find peace. Sleep becomes my way to cope and survive. If only it were possible to sleep twenty-four-seven. But it is not.

CHAPTER 19

A Glimpse of Love

Tiny, petite, and full of energy, Judy brought life into my world. We met at Cubberley Elementary in fifth grade. Although we seemed to be complete opposites in most ways, a friendship between us grew. While I was quiet and shy, Judy was a leader: confident, quick-witted, and very smart.

Physically well developed for a sixth grader, Judy seemed beyond her years. Like me, she had older siblings, which may have contributed to her being so mature for her age. Often we would walk home from Cubberley Elementary together, and I would walk the extra mile or so out of my way to stop at her house. I was guaranteed two pieces of white bread with a slice of American cheese between them, which was well worth the extra mile.

Wearing a house dress and apron, Judy's mom was always nearby. Pushing around a large dust mop, she kept her eye on us. She didn't like us making any messes. Unlike my house, their house was spotless. In Judy's bedroom everything had a place. In her closet a specific outfit hung for every day of the week. Monday, Tuesday, Wednesday, etc., were precisely hung and evenly spaced about three inches apart. Monday was a white pleated skirt with a pink angora sweater. Tuesday was a black skirt with a white blouse and short black sweater, and so on.

Besides being meticulously clean, her home was full of music. Dave, her older brother, had a large reel-to-reel tape player that held an enormous collection of oldies but goodies. Judy and I would sit and listen and watch as the fast-forward winding of the tape landed on our song request. Dave patiently moved from one song request to the next until, eventually, the visit came to an end. Judy's mom handed me my coat and books and encouraged me out the front door. It was time for me to go home.

Judy was heads above me when it came to matters of the heart. There was always a cute boy she had a crush on. There were even days I was uninvited to walk home with her, missing out on the desired cheese sandwich, because her latest flame was walking her home.

She had no secrets, revealing she had kissed a few of her heartthrobs. Kissing! Judy offered to give me my first instructions about kissing.

"Come over here." One day she guided me to a grassy spot between her house and the house next door.

Hidden by a large hibiscus bush, we sat on the grass. Judy began the kissing demonstration by slowly and gently kissing the back of her hand. Over and over she repeated the demonstration and then told me to try it on my hand. I did.

Judy set her mind on orchestrating my first kiss. In sixth grade, she had an older boyfriend who had a brother our age. She encouraged her boyfriend to introduce me to his younger brother, Jerry. Jerry immediately took to me, but there was zero mutual attraction. One day, fumbling around, he awkwardly leaned toward me for a kiss. I wasn't having it! Extremely uncomfortable, I stiffened up and turned away, even though I felt tremendous pressure to follow Judy's mouth steps.

The arranged romance fizzled before it even got started, leaving Judy frustrated.

"Why don't you like him? He is so cute! You know he was going to kiss you!"

Judy had no idea what went on at my house and what was behind my timid reluctance to comingle with any boy. One day I decided to confide in her about Don calling me into his bedroom. She looked at me like I had just created a whopper of a story and burst into laughter. It would be the last time I would ever try to explain to her or anyone else what was going on in my house.

Best of friends, we graduated from Cubberley, and now we are beginning Marshall Junior High School together. If she is nervous, it doesn't show. She carries herself with confidence and is always perfectly put together. Her chestnut-brown hair is teased and shaped into a flawless bubble bouffant, making her seem taller. Her well-developed figure and pretty outfits draw attention from everyone. Boys gravitate toward her. I am an observer and admirer of her poised demeanor. Maybe even a little envious.

Large-leafed maple trees line Wardlow Road, offering a little shelter from the warm afternoon sun. Judy and I chat about our day as we walk home from school, comparing our homework assignments. Now in ninth grade, even Judy with her gifted intelligence is feeling the weight of her accelerated classes.

Unexpectedly, a lowered blue Chevy pulls up to the curb, and the driver calls out, "Hey, Judy." From the sidewalk I am sure I recognize him. His name is Terry. He is an older guy, a friend of my sister Christine, and has been to our house several times. Laughing and gesturing with her hands, Judy chitchats through the car window. After Terry drives off, Judy giddily tells me she has a date with him on Saturday night.

Saturday comes, and at midday Judy and I walk to the Golden Lantern, a neighborhood fast food hangout right across from Millikan High School. We order a Coke and find a table to sit at. Surprised, Judy points to the line of people at the service window. Terry is standing in line with a good friend, Pat. When they get their order, they come over and sit with us at our table. Judy, cool and composed, can talk to anyone with ease. I sit tongue-tied as the three of them laugh and chat. What happens next I don't see coming.

Terry blurts out, "Hey, why don't you and Pat come with us tonight? We could double date!"

Judy, unaware my heart is nervously beating out of my chest, immediately chimes in, "Yes! Yes! That would be so much fun."

I am too shy and slow to conjure up a story to get myself out of the horrifying situation. Making things worse, I am certain Pat must be feeling awkward too.

After lunch Judy and I walk back to my house. I am panic stricken and feel physically ill at the thought of the predicament I have gotten myself into. I want to run and retreat to the safety of my bedroom.

"I have nothing to wear, Judy! Nothing!"

Mom happens to be home and must have recognized the panic on my face. Sensitive to my predicament, she immediately drives to nearby Zody's and buys me a pair of black stirrup pants. Judy lends me her beautiful pink angora sweater. Unexpectedly and surprisingly, excitement begins to edge out my panic and fear. Judy and I giggle as we get ready for our big dates. Terry and Pat are eighteen, and we are just fourteen. *How could he want to take me out?* I keep thinking to myself.

At six o'clock, Pat and Terry show up at my front door. I am surprised to see Pat is driving and not Terry. He has a lowered, 1957 aqua-green Pontiac. Terry and Judy climb into the back seat, nuzzled up side by side. Pat opens the passenger-side door, and I climb in. My intuition tells me I am supposed to scoot over and sit next to him, so I do.

Something about Pat makes my heart flutter. He isn't very tall. He has brown, wavy hair combed into a small pompadour that adds an inch or so to his height. Dressed in a brown pullover V-necked sweater pulled over a white T-shirt, he is handsome, and, an added bonus, he smells heavenly.

The radio is cranked up, blasting familiar tunes. The three of them are singing, laughing, and joking, filling the car with an exuberant energy. Our first stop is at an outdoor go-kart facility. We each climb into our own assigned go-kart, and the challenge is on as to who will beat whom. Firmly gripping the small steering wheel, I let out a burst of nervous laughter. With my foot pressed fiercely on the gas pedal, my heart is in it to win it. Unimaginable, but I manage to take up the rear at each turn. Regardless of my slow pace, I am having a blast.

The waving of a white flag signifies our allotted time has come to an end as we are directed to an area where we park the go-karts. It is obvious who the winner is, and it isn't me. What is also obvious is my zipper has exploded in my new stirrup pants. Frantic, I try to cover my exposed panties with my hands. Pat quickly realizes I am having problems and hands me his jacket to wrap around my waist. "Thank you!" I smile and feel relieved. His quick response helps make the embarrassing situation easy, and his kindness is touching.

It is a perfect, warm California evening. Windows down, with the sweet sea smell of the ocean in the air and music blaring, Pat drives along Pacific Coast Highway to Huntington Beach. I'm in unfamiliar territory, but I'm enjoying myself. Finally we arrive at our destination and park. As if he has known me for some time, Pat takes hold of my hand while we walk to a small venue right on Main Street, called the Golden Bear. To my surprise I welcome his touch.

Barely past the front entrance, we are squished together like sardines in a can. The Golden Bear is packed. The atmosphere is electric as we nudge our way into the crowd full of high-spirited energy. Pat never lets go of my hand, leading us deeper into the crowd.

The enticing music is booming, making it almost impossible to talk to each other. Inching our way forward, I notice a small raised stage in front of us. The artist behind the microphone is garish, dazzling the crowd with her throaty, raw voice. Finally I can see her small frame. She is decked out in flowy bell-bottoms and a short-sleeve, quilted vest. Her arms are bejeweled with numerous jangles, and her long, wild, crazy hair is flying about while she fiercely belts out soulful songs. She is messy, but at the same time, there is something magical and beautiful about her. I am mesmerized

Golden Bear (web photo)

by her uninhibited, gritty performance. I learn her name: Janis Joplin.

Singing, dancing, and clapping, we are immersed in the crowd's magnetic buzz and her exhilarating voice for over an hour. I look around the room, soaking in the pulsing energy. I have never experienced anything like this. Mystifyingly I feel connected to everyone around me and especially to Pat.

My first date is perfect. It just seems to go by too quickly. The date I had dreaded I now don't want to end. During the drive back to my house, Terry and Judy are very quiet in the back seat. *Probably kissing,* I think to myself. Pat begins to ask me some questions. "So did you have a good time tonight?" My response is a soft, shy, "Yes."

Finally we park in front of my house, and together we walk up to my front porch. "Well, I had a great time," he says as he boldly looks straight into my eyes. He surprises me, placing both of his hands firmly, but gently on my face. Leaning into me he places his mouth on mine. His lips are full and soft, and the kiss is tender and lingers. My body tingles in response.

"Oh! She is not only beautiful, but she can kiss!" he blurts out with a little laughter.

I open the door, step into the house, and say, "Good night." As soon as the door closes behind me, I lean against it. I touch my lips with the tips of my fingers and close my eyes. *My first kiss!* I think to myself as I savor every second of Pat's touch.

One date, and I feel smitten with this handsome boy. He is cute and funny, and he said I am beautiful and a good kisser! That night I curl up in bed and replay every part of our date. I think about how wonderful he smells and feel ever so grateful Judy had taught me about kissing. I fall asleep easily that night. It is a deep, peaceful sleep, the kind I can't remember having.

My utopia doesn't last long. My sister Christine hears I went out with Pat Coakley, and she doesn't like it one bit. She warns me he is a player and too old for me.

"He is very popular and can have any girl he wants. He has a new girlfriend every other month. You are going to get hurt! Don't even think about seeing him again." Her words scare me, but they can't squelch the spark that has been ignited inside me.

The next day a girl identifying herself as Debbie calls me. Through tears she tells me she has been dating Pat and is pregnant with his baby.

"Please don't go out with him again," she asks desperately.

Her words pour cold water on the spark within me, and I decide my sister is right. I promise Debbie I won't go out with him again. A day or so later, Pat calls me. He invites me to go out for a second date the following Saturday.

Softly I tell him, "No, I can't."

His silence confirms my response took him by surprise. A young fourteen-year-old girl declining to go out with him again!

"Why not?" he finally asks.

I am honest and tell him about the phone call I had received from Debbie. He is furious and tells me he hasn't dated her in a long time. Shortly after, I receive another call from Debbie. Through more tears she recants her story. She isn't pregnant and apologizes for the trouble she has caused.

Our dates increase, and mutual affection blossoms. Regardless of our age difference, he seems proud to introduce me to his friends. One night he asks me if I want to meet his parents. We drive to his house on Studebaker a little after ten o'clock. His parents had already retired for the evening but tell us to come into their bedroom where they are watching TV. I follow Pat, and he introduces me to his lovely parents. They are very friendly, but their kind greeting doesn't hide the surprise and concern I see in their faces. My hypervigilant nature gives me the ability to be a good reader of people. Pat later tells me they were very concerned about our age difference.

Because Mom is gone on weekends, Pat and I have a lot of alone time. We spend many hours lying next to each other on my sofa. Johnny Mathis serenades us with his soothing, romantic voice. "It's Not for Me to Say" revolves in a circle on the phonograph while I press my face into his neck and the scent of his cologne imprints into my senses. With his arms wrapped around me, we spend hours cradled together. I listen to him breathe and feel his heartbeat. Often we both fall asleep. It is a first for me, to feel safe and loved and let someone of the opposite sex so close to me. Sensual feelings are stirred, and I feel joy, not dirty.

Pat is my first love, that special person who has touched my life and will forever be a part of me. Handsome, with a great sense of humor, he makes me feel beautiful, desired, and safe. For eight months he is consistently in my world—eight months enveloped in something I have never experienced. A whole new world opens up for me. I let my protective walls drop and allow myself to feel. I am introduced to emotions I have never known before…wonder, excitement, and many physical firsts. I live every day for my next connection with Pat. When I wake up, I think of him. When I go to bed, I think of him.

Soon I learn the person who has brought me so much comfort and happiness will also shatter my heart. It is subtle, but I sense a change. He starts skipping our usual evenings together. When we do spend the evening together, our time is often cut short. He calls less and less and less and less. A combination of things, maybe? Parental pressures, our age difference, and other life forces and ambitions finally come between us. I learn Pat joined the air force and went to Louisiana for his basic training.

It is not easy letting go. I sleep with and cling to a sweater Pat had left at my house, breathing in traces of his scent. The loss of his tender touch, his voice, his laughter, his attention, and the loss of being with someone who makes me feel I am beautiful and special devastates me. I am lost in a world of pain for some time. I learn a lot from my first love. I learn about a tenderness I didn't know existed, and I learn where there is love, there is also great pain.

CHAPTER 20

Blank Check

Ninth grade comes to a welcomed end. The loss of my relationship with Pat leaves me further emotionally frayed and impacts my already hindered abilities to function at school. It is almost impossible. Soon I will be starting Millikan High School.

I don't know how I manage it, but entering high school, I am placed in accelerated classes. It will be a curse—a formidable challenge I cannot measure up to. Skipping school becomes a compulsive norm. Being alone and bidding for sleep are the only ways I can find relief.

High school brings greater intellectual and social expectations as well. There are sororities, school clubs, social events, dances, and social pressures, especially dating, which adds to my anxiety.

My desire to please and do well is at war with my emotional shackles. I awaken in the morning with a tiny spark of desire to get up, get dressed, and go to school. My self-talk, "You can do this!" isn't enough to overcome the hidden battles I fight. Most days the spark is easily snuffed out by my need to cocoon myself from my pain.

It is Monday, and I have determined I am going to go to school and turn things around. I have not been to school in maybe two or three weeks. I have lost count. I enter my first period, feeling sheepish, knowing many eyes are on me, aware of how much school I have missed. Settling in, it isn't long before my teacher hands me a note to report to Vice Principal DuBois's office.

There are several chairs in the waiting room of Mr. DuBois's office. They are exactly the same—slender, mahogany wood with worn brown tweed cushions. Everything in his office is familiar to me, since I have been summoned here numerous times after lengthy absences. I make my way to the middle chair situated next to a window that looks out onto a row of oak trees centered in a wide stretch of grass. In the distance I can see students gathered in distinct clusters chatting. *Probably talking about their latest flame or newest angora sweater,* I think to myself.

I can't help but wonder what it is about me that doesn't fit in. Watching them laughing and having fun from this distance, I usually feel a sense of safety, but not today. My stomach churns as I anticipate facing Mr. DuBois after missing so much school.

The door to his office gently opens.

Mr. DuBois has always been kind and supportive. I hate myself for letting him down. He motions for me to come in. Nervous, I quickly sit in the chair in front of his desk. As I focus on an eight-by-ten photograph of him and his family, I wonder, *What would it be like to have a dad like him?*

Mr. DuBois takes his place across from me on the other side of his desk. The next few moments linger uncomfortably. Then his voice breaks the silence. "Kathy, you have been absent thirty days. This is the most consecutive days of absence yet."

Thirty days? I'm stunned it has been that many. After a few more lingering moments of silence, he picks up a pen and begins to write on a small piece of paper. In large bold letters, he pens the words BLANK CHECK.

"Kathy, this is a blank check. You can use it at any time to get back into school. No questions will be asked, and you will know when the time is right."

I think I see tears welling up in his eyes as he reaches over his desk and places the piece of paper in my hand. Folding the paper in half, I tuck it into the pocket of my coat and quietly say, "Thank you."

It was the last time I would ever see Mr. DuBois. After that it becomes more and more difficult to get myself to school. Now, at fifteen, I have fallen seriously behind, making it almost impossible to catch up. I carry around a dreadful weight of shame for being such a failure. For a brief time, Mom enrolls me in an alternative school. A friend, Bridget, goes there so I'm willing to give it a try. The school is a conglomerate of white, black, and Hispanic kids. We are each certainly unique with different stories, but we have one thing in common: we can't cut it in the traditional school setting.

One day I ride the bus home with Jerome, a black kid who is a year older than me. Jerome has always been friendly to me, and I like him. He is a talker but often speaks fast and in slang I don't always understand. As is usual for me, when he talks, I nod my head in agreement with a little smile. Before approaching my stop to exit the bus, Jerome places a thick, rolled-up cigarette in my hand. "You be cool!" he says as I exit the bus. I place the rolled stubby cigarette in my pocket. When I get home, I set it on the kitchen counter and think maybe Mom or someone else will want it, because I don't have any plans to start smoking. The stuff hits the fan when Mom gets home and sees it.

"Where the hell did this come from?"

I get the third-degree interrogation. The answers are simple and truthful. I had no idea it was marijuana.

I don't seem to fit in at the alternative school either. While I am depressed and withdrawn, a lot of the kids at the school are rough, rude, and brash. Several times I watch kids getting into loud arguments where venom spews and the four-letter "F word" flies loosely. I am surprised the teachers seem to ignore this kind of behavior, almost fearful of intervening.

Now in school limbo, I find myself even more isolated. Mom is able to get me enrolled back at Millikan, but it doesn't change my inner turmoil or my attendance.

* * *

Mom turns the Styrofoam cup upside down, and all her tips tumble onto the kitchen table. With her finger she separates the coins, pushing all the quarters toward me so I can group them into fours. Suddenly our alone time is interrupted. Out of the blue, a group of girls from Zeus, a sorority at Millikan High School, bursts into our kitchen. Loud cheering and giggles fill the small room. I recognize a few of the faces, Frances, Danilyn, Tina, and a couple of others whom I'd known since Cubberley Elementary.

As they take up every inch of the kitchen and applaud exuberantly, it slowly begins to sink in what is happening. They are kidnapping me and making me an honorary member. In the midst of all the commotion, I can see on Mom's face she has been in on the surprise and is happy for me…maybe even hoping this will be the catalyst for helping me go to school. I am stunned. Overwhelmed and speechless, I have no idea how it all works. "Grab some clothes and your toothbrush. Come on, hurry!" I am instructed to grab a few things, and then I'll get whisked off to spend the night at a slumber party with the sorority members of Zeus. Since I'm very good at putting on a happy face, no one will ever notice my unease.

This sudden surprise opens a new chapter in my life, a chapter that will bring someone into my world who, together with me, will create two of the biggest blessings I could ever imagine.

CHAPTER 21

The New Chapter

Tina, the president of Zeus, delivers the invitation to me.
"All the new officers will be sworn in, and new members will take an oath and be recognized. It is a very special occasion. Even honorary members of Zeus must go through the installation ceremony. It is a lot of fun, and everyone dresses up and brings a date."

Oh my gosh, what do I do? A date? My mind is spinning in a panic. Then I remember. I remember the guy I met a few months earlier. A friend since grade school invited me to join a group of Zeus girls in an annual gathering of Millikan High School sororities and fraternities. Now that I think about it, maybe that weekend prompted my kitchen to be flooded with lovely Zeus girls and my surprise honorary membership.

The annual gathering customarily takes place in the uniquely beautiful town of Big Bear. Surrounded by the San Bernardino National Forest, Big Bear is a year-round playground, and the young masses of teenagers take to it well. Reserving most of the cabins in the town, the fraternities and sororities turn the small town into a party scene for an entire weekend.

It was beautiful Mary Louise whom Louie had his eyes on. Gathered in our small, warm, cozy cabin, his interest was obvious. Vying for her attention, he dished out compliments in droves.

"You are so beautiful!" he said, trying to flatter her, but I'm not sure he realized she already had a date for the night.

I mused silently while brushing my hair. Shortly Mary's date arrived, and off they went. Louie instantly bounced back and asked me if he could take over brushing my hair. I didn't feel threatened. After all, it wasn't me he was interested in, so I responded, "Sure."

Immediately Louie put me at ease. He was funny and easy to be around. We talked, laughed, and just hung out for a couple of hours.

Now needing a date, I remember our brief time together at Big Bear. I muster up the courage and ask him if he will go with me to the installation ceremony. He says yes.

And so it begins. Louie asks me out a few more times, and then the call comes. Many of his high school buddies who had also joined the military receive the same call—to serve our country in a controversial war: Vietnam.

It is a somber drive from Long Beach to Camp Pendleton, in San Diego, as I sit in the car with near-perfect strangers. Nana, Louie's grandmother, has flown in from Pennsylvania to see her grandson off, and I am also invited to go with the family.

"Kathy, would you like to join us in sending Louie off?" Mr. Hockel had asked me. I had only met Mr. and Mrs. Hockel a few times, but I responded, "Yes, of course, I would."

Arriving at Camp Pendleton, we check in through a security gate and are assigned a visitor pass. Louie meets us, proudly wearing a marine khaki service uniform. Seeing him in uniform makes the situation seem that much more factual. He isn't the young man I'm used to seeing in jeans and a T-shirt.

He is a marine, and he is going off to war. He gives us a quick tour, and as we walk around, I note how everything is pristine, nothing out of place. The environment is cold, just like the mood in each of us. As the tour continues, we smile, but the heaviness we each feel is undeniable…especially Lou Senior. I can see Mr. Hockel struggling to place a smile over the horrific weight of his concerns.

As I observe Mr. Hockel, I think to myself, *This moment is a zillion moments away from the young boy he bounced around on his back for pony rides, a zillion moments away from the young boy he taught to look both ways when he crossed the street, a zillion moments away from the challenging young boy the nuns corrected with the sharp whack of a ruler, and a zillion moments away from the young man he taught to drive.* I survey the room, and stiff, sad faces are everywhere. All of these young men are being shipped off to a war zone over seven thousand miles from family and home.

Shortly we are ushered into a large mess hall, where they provide us dinner, but eating is the last thing I feel like doing. A soft chatter hums throughout the room as families mingle together. Taking it all in, I wonder what the conversations might be at each table. What do you talk about the night you send your child off to war?

Soon, way too soon, the moment I have been dreading has arrived. It is time to say our goodbyes. My heart heavy, I stand awkwardly, clustered together with Louie's family. I can no longer hear the hubbub of the other families surrounding us. No one is laughing or telling stories—just somber faces everywhere. Louie's mom, although she is not a big hugger, wraps her arms around her son. Next Nana moves toward her grandson. She wipes a few tears from her eyes and gives him a big hug.

"Loubird, you are going to be fine, my grandson."

I can hear her every word, and I know Loubird is the special nickname she gave him as a child. I try to swallow the lump in my throat because I know it is my turn. It seems right that Mr. Hockel will be the last one to say his goodbyes. Facing Louie, I step forward. I wrap my arms around him, and we hug for a good length of time. We haven't known each other that long, but still, caught up in the moment, I wonder if I will ever see him again. I wonder how many of these young men will come home and how many won't.

"Please write when you can," I softly say to him.

Mr. Hockel, trying hard to stuff his emotions, grabs his son and gives him a pep talk. "You are going to be fine, son. You are going to be fine. Contact us as soon as you can. We love you, son." His voice cracks, and I can see he doesn't want to let go of his eldest son, cherishing every second of their embrace.

Louie is smiling bravely, trying hard to hold it all together, mostly for his family, but finally he lets go of his dad, and we all have to part ways. I want to escape the weight of the gloom clinging to me, but I'm compelled to look back. I see Louie standing in the spot we left him, watching his family walk away. My insides are aching, churning with sadness hovering all around me. The war in Vietnam is new to me, new to all of us, and yet already an ominous speculative fear has infiltrated our lives. *Will he be okay? Will we see him again?*

Mr. Hockel unlocks the car doors, I climb in the back seat with Nana, and Mrs. Hockel takes the front passenger seat. Even in the dark, I can see Mr. Hockel standing right outside the car near my window. I can hear him sobbing. It is all so overwhelming. Finally after a few minutes, he climbs into the driver's seat and starts the car. No one talks the entire two-hour drive home, and tears continue to flow from Mr. Hockel. There is nothing anyone can say or do to console him.

My first letter from Louie arrives, and it is thirty-four pages. Louie wrote daily on the ship and gives in-depth details of his daily activities. It is like him to inject humor into everything, except the end of his letters always takes a more serious turn. He shares how much he misses me, how beautiful I am, and to please write. Letters are his lifeline to home.

One way of communicating with family during the war is to send cassette recordings back and forth. One day Mr. Hockel calls and invites me for dinner. "Hi Kath, we would like to have you come for dinner, and when we are done eating, we'll have you record a message to Louie, and we will send it off to him."

Dinner is delicious even though I'm not exactly sure what I'm eating…some type of meat and vegetables and something else. After dinner Mr. Hockel takes me into a small bedroom, where a cassette player is set up. He gives me some quick instructions on how to use it, then leaves the room, closing the door behind him. Alone in the room, I think about what I am going to say. Ready or not I push the on button and begin to talk.

"Your parents are so nice to invite me for dinner. It was delicious—meat and peas and carrots and something else (I don't know what it was exactly), but everything was really good. I hope you are doing okay and are staying safe. I enjoy your letters and will try to write as often as possible. Please take care of yourself. Bye, Louie." I push the stop button. Oh my gosh!

It went so fast! Did I say enough? Did I talk too fast? My heart racing, I feel flustered, but it is done, and there is nothing I can change even if I want to.

A few weeks later, Mr. Hockel calls and invites me for dinner again. "Hi Kath, can you come for dinner? We want to send Louie another message."

I gently knock on the kitchen door right off their driveway.

"Come on in Kath—dinner is all ready."

Mouthwatering aromas fill the kitchen, and I can see the table is all set. Mr. Hockel points for me to sit in the same chair I sat in during my last visit. Mrs. Hockel serves the best fried chicken I have ever tasted and delicious homemade iced tea. It isn't long before Mr. Hockel tells me, "Oh Kathy, by the way, last time you came for dinner, we had a pork roast, and that was rice we had with it."

I feel my face turn a little flushed. I had never eaten pork roast or rice before, but now I know I like it. Also, it dawns on me that whatever I say on the taped message will be listened to. This is something I hadn't thought about. After dinner Mr. Hockel once again takes me to the small bedroom and leaves me alone to record my message. I pull a piece of paper out of my pocket and slowly read the message into the recorder. When I am done, I push the stop button and breathe a sigh of relief. Finished, I open the door to the bedroom, and Mr. Hockel is standing right outside the door, in the hallway, waiting for me.

One day while I'm sitting at home, the phone rings. I pick up the receiver, and a telephone operator asks me if I will accept a call from Private Louis Hockel. Completely surprised, I answer, "Yes, of course!"

A phone patch is made through MARS, and although a little garbled and distant, I soon hear Louie's voice. "Hi Kate," then he adds, "Over."

Silly me, I respond, "Where are you?" There is a long pause until I realize I need to say, "Over."

The phone call is nerve-racking and doesn't feel natural. Still it is good to hear Louie's voice and to know he is okay. The MARS system offers soldiers and sailors a way to communicate with their families and loved ones back home. Louie has only five minutes, and it goes by fast. All the "overs" take up some of that cherished time.

Louie is deployed for an entire year. He writes to me often, and I am happy to respond. Miles and miles apart, our relationship grows through handwritten words on paper. It is safe to write sweet things on a piece of paper, especially when the recipient is so far away. The many "I miss yous" and compliments tug at my heartstrings. "Unchained Melody" by the Righteous Brothers becomes our song, and my feelings flourish in a make-believe way.

Louie has a knack for making me laugh. The five-by-seven brown envelope that arrives is much different from the usual small white envelopes I'm used to receiving from him. Eagerly I open it and find my own personal cassette message. Excited, I grab my newly purchased cassette player, insert the tape, and push play.

"Greg, help me. Your Aunt Kathy put me in this box, and I can't get out. Help! Help! Please help me get out of this box, Greg."

My five-year-old nephew's big brown eyes open wide as saucers. Puzzled, he examines every inch of the tape player looking for Louie. Frantic, he suddenly shouts, "Get him out of the box, Aunt Kathy! Get him out!" It takes me a good amount of time to convince him Louie is okay.

Louie's letters are funny and encouraging and make me feel special. I also know the ones I write are important to him and help him get through his long days. Letters are helpful to several of his other friends too, some on the front lines of combat.

Anxiously I wait for the mailman. He consistently delivers the mail around twelve-thirty. Soon I hear him outside as he inserts the mail through the mail slot on the front door. Mail scatters all over the floor. I scramble through the envelopes searching for a letter from Louie. There it is! I grab the letter, quickly open it, and begin reading.

"Hi Kate, how are you doing? How is Greg? Does he still think I'm locked in a box?" I stop and grin because my sweet nephew continues to stare at my cassette player and ask, "Is Louie inside the box, Aunt Kathy?"

I continue reading…"I've got some bad news. Big K was shot." My heart drops. Worried, I anxiously read on. "The good news is he is on a military hospital ship outside of Chu Lai where I'm stationed. Being the stud that I am, I was able to type up some orders for myself and hitch a ride on a helicopter to the USS *Sanctuary* in the Red China Sea. He is going to be okay. It was really good to see him, and you should have seen his face. They had him upright, resting in a chair reading a *Reader's Digest*, when I snuck up behind him and got really close. Close enough to tick him off. Then from behind, I whispered in his ear, 'I'm a monkey. Let's party!' When he realized it was me, we had a good laugh, and damn it was so good to see him!" I stop reading and can picture the two of them enjoying this glorious reunion so far from home, and I also wonder what the heck "I'm a monkey" means. I start reading again.

Big K & Louie

"Hey, time flew by and soon I realized I'd better get my arse back to Chu Lai. Luck would have it, General Leonard Cushman was on board the USS *Sanctuary* giving Purple Hearts to some of the wounded. As his huge helicopter revved up, I knew I had to get on it with his entourage. Last time Kenny saw me I was shaking hands with the general aboard his chopper. I told him the story of my best friend getting wounded and how I hitched a ride to see him. General Cushman is a fighting man's general, with numerous merits for bravery, so he applauded my surprise visit and was more than happy to take a little detour back to my camp!" Laughing and shaking my head as I read Louie's account, the whole ordeal sounds just like something he could pull off. "General Cushman's entourage alerted the gunnery sergeant at the camp in Chu Lai that they would be making a visit. Mayhem ensued as the gunnery had everyone running around spit shining the camp the best they could in the brief allotted time to prepare for General Cushman's visit. The gunnery was not one bit happy with me, but I didn't care."

Later Big K sent me a letter and I learned he recouped on the USS *Sanctuary* for just over a month. The warm baths, blue pajamas, bed with clean sheets, hot meals, and American nurses were reminiscent of home and safety, yet he could not shake his buddies still fighting back on the hill in Khe Sahn. He had to get back to them, and get back to them he did.

* * *

The hideous impact of the war strikes close to home again—just around the corner on Carfax. I notice some neighbors down the street put up a large flagpole in their front yard and raise the American flag to half-mast. Their only son, Steve, won't be coming home. *How can this be? He is too damn young!* I remember it wasn't that long ago his front yard was full of family and friends celebrating his high school graduation. A cluster of balloons and a *Congratulations* sign were displayed in the same front yard now flying the American flag at half-mast.

* * *

During the year Louie is gone, I get further and further behind in school. Mom is gone, staying with Don on weekends. With no parents around, the word soon spreads that our house is the place to hang out. Especially on weekends our house has a steady flow of fun seekers.

I glance in the mirror, taking one last look at myself. It is almost six o'clock on Friday. I'm expecting Louie's younger brother, Greg, who is my age, and his buddies, Kelly and Scott. Downing a few beers is the precursor to checking into the Friday night Millikan High School dance at Eldorado Park Canteen. My house is the perfect place.

Scott, sporting a permed afro and having mastered the smooth moves of The Temptations, gyrates enthusiastically around our small living room as "Ain't Too Proud To Beg" reverberates from the Magnavox console. Kelly, small in stature, lacks nothing in personality. He is outgoing and hilarious. Greg, smart and good-looking, is my link to the three of them…"the Trifecta—Triple Threat."

Mocking Scott's smooth dance moves, Kelly does his own exaggerated soulful version of the Motown group across the living room to the phonograph and switches up the record to "Baby I Need Your Lovin'." With beers in hand, the four of us loudly belt out in unison…

"Baby I need your lovin',
Got to have all your lovin'!

Some say it's a sign of weakness
For a man to beg
Then weak I'd rather be
If it means having you to keep
Cause lately I've been losing sleep
Baby I need your lovin'!
Got to have all your lovin'!"

As the Friday night beer buzz gathering continues, camaraderie, music, and laughter spill over into my world. Partaking in a little brew fosters the release of my inhibitions. "Twist and Shout" is the next forty-five RPM dropped beneath the needle on the phonograph. I jump onto a chair and feel the music move through me! "Shake it up baby, now! Shake it up!" The beer, music, and lyrics all evoke confidence and abandon. Letting go of my fears for a mere couple of hours, I feel like I belong. I feel accepted—like one of the gang. We continue to drink, sing, and dance until...

"See you later, Kath. We gotta go."

The party ends as the guys shift their focus to the clock and getting to the dance. Hugs, thank-yous, and tidying up are imparted, and then the three of them rush out the door waving goodbye. And just like that, the music stops.

Alcohol becomes a friend, a vehicle that allows me to let down protective walls and override my insecurities. A few beers and I discover a new side of myself, a young girl who loves to have fun, laugh, and encourage others to join in.

Sandy, also known as Hendy or "Iron Pants," as she is dubbed because she unapologetically guards her virginity, is several years older than me. She has graduated from high school, has her own car—a tan VW Bug—and a job. When she isn't working, we are hanging out. The green roll of five dollars Mom leaves me for the weekend seems to be just enough to help with gas money, some beer, and a Len's burger. Sandy's free-spirited nature is the perfect complement to the part of me that longs to be uninhibited.

Midmorning I look out the kitchen window just as Sandy pulls up in front of my house in her VW Bug with the music blasting. Adorned in my white feather hat, a sleeveless shift dress over my bikini, and my beach bag, which holds a hairbrush, beach towel, the infamous iodine baby oil tanning mixture, and my green roll of dimes, I'm ready to go.

"Let's get a Len's burger. I'm starving!" she hollers over the booming lyrics of "Groovin' on a Sunday Afternoon" as I climb into her car.

A huge smile covers her face as she quickly shifts the Bug into first, second, and third gear. We are off. There is no chatter between us, just singing. With the windows rolled down and the wind blowing on our faces, we are without a care in the world. We cruise through Lakewood to Len's for one of their delicious burgers and then on to Belmont Shore.

There is never a dull moment hanging out with Sandy. Whether we find ourselves partying at Franklin's condo, dancing in the back of his El Camino, or camping at Strawberry Fields, we always find or create a great time. The entire year Louie is deployed to Vietnam, Sandy and I are joined at the hip. For me it is a year of embracing new freedoms and added deterrents from school.

Through our letters I confide to Louie about school and how I am thinking of dropping out. "No, Kate, you need to stick it out and finish." The entire year he is gone, he does his best to steer me in a positive direction. It isn't enough.

When I am almost seventeen, my mom signs the necessary papers for me to quit school. She had done the same for Christine, so maybe this failure is a little easier for her to swallow…a way of saying, "Oh well. She'll have to figure it out."

It is a beautiful day. I open the front door to let the warmth escape through the screen door. I push the vacuum all around our avocado-green carpet, only occasionally stopping to pull out the spiked burrs wedged into the fibers. Suddenly something catches my attention. Standing on our front porch, on the other side of the screen door, Louie is dressed in his full marine uniform. I drop the vacuum, push the door open, and wrap my arms around him. He is home!

A safe return home from a war zone is unquestionably a reason to celebrate. Just home from Vietnam, Kenny, Dave, Louie, and others gather at the Hockels' home, drinking beer and telling stories old and new. Well after midnight the party slows down except for a couple of diehards.

It is almost two in the morning, and I have long gone to bed. I'm deep asleep and immersed in a dream, but loud cries of "Quack! Quack!" reverberate throughout my bedroom. Now only half asleep, I consider that I must be dreaming about ducks. Abruptly the deafening "Quack! Quack! Quack!" is obtrusively close. Dazed and confused, I'm awakened and sit up in bed.

"Louie, I am going to kill you!" Mom hollers, while wildly swinging a broom out my bedroom window, aiming at some poor innocent duck's head half protruding into my room.

I'm totally perplexed by what I see. Mom is trying to whack a duck whose head is half in my bedroom window while someone is laughing in the distance.

"Quack! Quack! Quack!" the noisy duck call continues undeterred.

Another strong-minded swing with the broom, and Mom's voice escalates. "You are on my shit list, Louie!"

After several more determined swings with the broom, finally the poor duck's head is pushed out of my window and disappears. For the next hour, the hooligans who captured the ducks from Eldorado Park drive by our house and continue to tirelessly yell out, "Quack! Quack! Quack!"

The next morning, tired out from the previous night's escapades, I curl up on the sofa giggling, trying to elicit a tinge of laughter out of Mom. She isn't having it. Then the phone rings.

"Kluck, do you have any idea how this duck got in my car? There is duck shit everywhere!" Mike Qualls, our neighbor, questions me on the other end of the phone. Recently he had purchased his treasured pride and joy: a lowered, pristine, candy-apple red Chevy from the guru of fine cars, Jerry Cohen. Needless to say, he was not the least bit pleased when he found a duck had defecated all over the interior of his most prized possession.

* * *

While Louie has a great bond with his buddies, we seem to click too. His humor helps me to feel at ease, and I am very drawn to his family. I soak in Mr. Hockel's warmth and kindness, and I can easily see the thread of humor in the family lead straight to him. Sitting around the dinner table, kibitzing, jokes flow abundantly.

I hear stories of him setting the clocks ahead an hour and then proceeding to drop the kids off at school an hour early. "Bye—have a good day," were his parting words as the kids approached a locked school before the sun rose. Retribution was imminent. Sitting around the table enjoying breakfast, the kids patiently waited for their dad to take his first delicious gulp of hot coffee, only to encounter a mouthful of dark molasses. Laughter erupted as he choked and spit out the cold, thick, syrupy concoction.

I think Mr. and Mrs. Hockel are a match made in heaven. Both equally short in stature, they love to dance, and boy they have smooth moves. They are part of the Greatest Generation, where a golden thread of music was the glue that fastened a nation together. Duke Ellington, Harry James, Benny Goodman, Glenn Miller, Tommy Dorsey, and countless songwriters and vocalists with extraordinary talents provided a common bond and joy through music during very difficult times—the Great Depression and WWII.

When "In the Mood" by Glen Miller is dropped onto the phonograph, it sends them stylishly gliding around the family living room. They are a sight to behold! They fit like a glove, and the charisma between them is magnetic. A coy grin covering Mrs. Hockel's face exudes happiness while her proud husband gently directs their moves.

Spending time with the Hockels introduces something extraordinary to my world. The warmth I see in their family awakens a yearning within me I didn't even know existed. The home-cooked family meals, the laughter, the music, and the affection all stir me. The more time I'm with them, the more welcome I feel and the more I'm captivated, especially by Louie's dad.

CHAPTER 22

Eighteen

Eighteen is a magical birthday for most adolescents. Crossing the bridge from childhood to adulthood, they are eager for more freedom and responsibilities. My eighteenth birthday is about four months away. I hadn't thought much about this upcoming milestone until one day when Mom shocks me with some news. Sitting around the kitchen table sorting her tips, she shares, "Don and I are going to sell the house. We want to get a place together. You are going to be eighteen and need to find some place to live."

Taken aback, I don't respond. The conversation ceases, and all is quiet around the kitchen table as I digest her words. I certainly don't feel excited about this milestone, and I certainly didn't plan on moving out on my own. In fact, the thought terrifies me.

Since quitting school I've had a couple of jobs that didn't last long. I worked at a fast-food place, but I encountered the same struggles. Feeling uncomfortable, fear clung to me, and escaping to the four walls of my bedroom and bidding for sleep eased my battle. I tried to follow in the steps of my mom and my sisters and got hired at Sixpense as a server. I was horrible at it, which heightened my unease. The real joy of my life has been kid-sitting my nephew, Greg—Janice and Ronnie's son. I started watching him several weeks after he was born, and he quickly became my little shadow, going everywhere with me. I adore him. However, even with the money I earn from babysitting, I struggle to pay my only bill—my car insurance for the 1958 VW Bug Mom bought me. Several times I've leaned on Louie to bail me out. Now I'm wondering how I am going to manage on my own.

With the weight of Mom's news on my mind, I offer to help Mrs. Hockel clear the table after another delicious dinner. "Thank you so much for dinner," I say after the dishes are done. Then Louie and I climb into his Fiat and drive just around the corner, to a hidden place under the freeway where we like to park. I can't shake what is on my mind. Overwhelmed and distracted, I finally tell him about Mom's plans.

"My mom is going to sell our house and move in with Don. I have to find someplace to move to." Louie doesn't shudder or wince. "We will get married." His response is that simple. "We will get married."

On January 25, 1969, Louie and I say our "I dos" in a small Methodist church. The special day arrives, and Frances, my maid of honor, and I rummage through my bedroom searching for my newly purchased high heels. On hands and knees, she delves into the pile of stuff under my bed.

"If you don't know where your wedding shoes are, you probably shouldn't be getting married!" Her words have zero humor attached to them.

Finally, I discover the shoe box sitting on a shelf in my closet. It contains the white heels to go with my wedding dress.

My wedding dress is on loan. A couple of months earlier, completely surprised, I received a call from a girl a couple of years older than me named Kathy (Zimmerman) Burnett.

"I heard you are getting married and might need a wedding dress. You are more than welcome to borrow mine."

The offer is extraordinarily generous—especially since I don't really even know Kathy. The dress arrives, and my heart is beating fast with anticipation. I have no idea what Kathy's dress looks like. Cautiously I unzip the long garment bag and carefully remove the gown. Truly elegant, the long-sleeve lace dress is beyond what I could have hoped for. Excited, I carefully step into the abundance of fabric. The fitted bodice hugs me perfectly, making my waist look tiny. The full lace skirt is grand. With an enormous smile, I twirl around like a princess at a ball. I feel beautiful.

So far I have been a bystander in all the wedding preparations. Mr. and Mrs. Hockel have generously paid for everything; they picked out and ordered invitations, the flowers, and the cake. They also planned a small reception at their home after the church reception. Mom offered to provide some alcohol for the reception at their home.

Mr. Hockel's words echoed in my ear.

"Kath, don't you think you should go tell your father in person that you are getting married?"

Surprised, I process his suggestion. *Maybe he is right*, I think to myself, trying to be open to the idea. I feel reluctant and uneasy, but I do want to ask him if he will walk me down the aisle.

It turns out my hesitancy was well-founded. Louie and I drive the two hours to Thousand Oaks, and after a cool greeting, we share our big news.

"Dad, Louie, and I are getting married in January and…"

I'm not able to finish my prepared speech before he interrupts.

"I hope you aren't wanting money. I can give you a hundred bucks, and that's it," he gruffly says.

Although I want to turn and run out the door, I begrudgingly respond, "No, I didn't come for money. I wanted to share our wedding plans and ask if you would walk me down the aisle."

"Sure, I'll walk you down the aisle," he retorts.

The visit is brief. On the drive home, I quietly chastise myself for even considering telling him in person. I want to curl up and make myself fall asleep, but I can't quiet the turmoil swirling through my mind. *I don't care if he walks me down the aisle! I'm not important to him. I should have never gone to his house.* Then I ruminate over how different my family is from Louie's.

CHAPTER 23

Marriage and Children

Southern California is having an unusually wet month. It has been raining for days. It's Friday, January 24, the evening of our wedding rehearsal, and our house is humming with chatter.

Louie's best friend, Big K, and Mom are kibitzing and laughing.

"You've got quite the swing, Sam."

I overhear Big K taunt Mom about her broom-swinging abilities, or lack of, all while he avidly denies any involvement in the duck-through-my-bedroom-window escapade.

Watching the clock, we wait for Harold to arrive so he can follow us to the church. With only ten minutes to get to the church, exasperated and concerned, Janice picks up the phone and calls him. He answers.

"Where are you? Are you okay? The wedding rehearsal starts in ten minutes!"

"It's pouring rain. I'm not driving in this weather; besides, I don't need a rehearsal. I'll be there tomorrow."

Janice's response is quick and sharp.

"You have one daughter who has asked you to walk her down the aisle, and you better show up!"

Our wedding day arrives—so does a lot more rain, and so does Harold. I must admit I'm relieved when I see he has arrived because I don't have a backup plan. And if in some corner of my heart I had held hope for some special words from him…it doesn't happen. Side by side we stand in the foyer of the church looking down the aisle, my stomach churning with nervous excitement. The small church is bursting with family and friends. I notice the overflow of attendees has been ushered onto the pulpit and instructed to sit in pews designated for the choir. The entire church is overflowing and then some.

I turn and take it all in, waiting for our cue to begin our walk down the aisle. Suddenly my sister Janice comes dashing in out of the rain with my nephew, Greg, in tow. My sweet nephew's big brown eyes are about to erupt with tears. With his sad face tugging at my heart, I lean down and wrap him up in my arms. "Aunt Kathy is not going anywhere, Greg. I love you!" He gives me a tiny smile, and soon Janice and Greg are ushered into the church.

The pastor presiding over our marriage is a cool dude. He often showed up five or ten minutes late to our premarriage counseling sessions casually dressed in shorts and flip flops. Louie, also inclined to show up in shorts and flip flops, took to him immediately. As we would stand outside the church door waiting for him, he would pull up in his convertible white T-Bird, jump out over the door, and greet us. Now I look down the aisle and see him donning a long black clergy robe, with Louie standing next to him in his formal white tux jacket and black slacks. A nervous giggle eeks out of me as they both look so uncomfortably handsome.

At two o'clock on January 25, 1969, I become Kathy Hockel. My heart is full of promise; I have joined a new family and have great dreams of creating my own.

* * *

The month of January continues to be wet and cold. Louie and I return from our weekend honeymoon in Las Vegas and begin to dive into unpacking and making the house on Carfax our own. Using Louie's veteran's loan benefit, we purchased the house from Mom for $17,000. We are stepping out on a financial limb, as our new house payment is $169 a month.

It is beyond strange to arrive home and have the house I grew up in completely empty and clean, except for our wedding gifts stacked neatly in a corner in my old bedroom.

One of our special gifts is a floor lamp with four beautiful candelabras that provides three levels of lighting: soft, medium, and bright. We purchased the lamp ourselves with some wedding money Nana gifted to us. While busy cleaning the house, Mom had hung the beautiful borrowed wedding dress on one of the candelabras. Heartbreakingly, the light was turned on, and the front bodice of the dress was scorched and burned. It seemed unthinkable that Kathy's dress could be ruined. Mom was heartsick when she discovered the tragedy. By the time I hear about the whole ordeal, Mom had taken the dress in for repair, and fortunately, through exquisite craftsmanship, Kathy's dress was repaired and dry cleaned to its near-original state. I don't know how they did it, but I am so thankful and relieved by the outcome.

Louie sets a box of new glasses on the kitchen counter. I wash and dry them and begin placing them in a cupboard. It is all new territory for me, arranging wedding gifts in my childhood home. While my sister Christine couldn't begin to comprehend how I could possibly consider purchasing this house with so many awful memories, I look at it as a new beginning for Louie and me. Also, being very good at not dealing with feelings, I push aside all the horror attached to the house. This is never more evident than when we make the bedroom Don and Mom occupied our bedroom. Over the next many months, we paint the inside and clean up the yard. Slowly the house on Carfax is getting a new face.

The year 1969 is a unique and crazy time in our country. Right before we are married, Richard Nixon is sworn in as the thirty-seventh president of the United States. Protests against the Vietnam War ramp up in the States, while at the same time unrelenting, bloody battles continue in 'Nam. One such battle in the dense jungles of the A Shau Valley of Vietnam, is called Hamburger Hill. The name is assigned to this battle due to the bitter fighting and high casualty rate. It raged on for ten days.

We are without a doubt a country divided by the Vietnam War. We are also a country divided on racial discrimination issues as exposed in the LA Watts riots, the Stonewall uprising in New York, and other unsettling tensions throughout the country.

A large mass of individuals with different ideas and values opposes the mainstream putative beliefs. In August of 1969, young long-haired hippies rebuff the establishment, seeking peace and love. With music, LSD, marijuana, and other drugs, they revel in glorious free love while promoting peace. During a three-day outdoor music festival called Woodstock, "Three Days of Peace and Music," the counterculture makes its enduring imprint on history.

The world in chaos and change around us, Louie and I are immersed in our little world. We decide to take our first postmarriage vacation. Excited, we pack our red VW Bug up tight and head out for breathtaking La Jolla Beach in Ensenada, Baja Mexico. We pass through town after town with music blaring, windows rolled down, and the fresh, sweet ocean air caressing our faces. The near-three-hour drive along the coast is beautiful and relaxing. Finally we arrive in San Diego and the border into Tijuana, Mexico. Crossing the border is pretty simple, but also a little intimidating. Mom's words loom in my mind.

"If you are ever arrested in Tijuana, you can kiss the USA goodbye!"

As we wait to be signaled through customs, numerous Mexican vendors of all ages approach us selling their goods. My eyes consume the young, dust-covered children in tattered clothes selling gum, candy, toys, and thin velvet blankets with large panthers imprinted on them.

Soon I realize making eye contact with them is an invitation for them to approach us with their wares. Torn between wanting to open our car doors and take them all home, or just hand them money, I am painfully aware we are entering a different country with different customs.

Finally we are through the hubbub at the border and are on our way. Another seventy-three miles, and we will be setting up our tent on a warm, white, sandy beach. I can't wait. Fishing, soaking in the rays, and partaking in authentic Mexican tacos from local street vendors, we enjoy the delicious food and drink, and our wonderful two-day getaway goes by too quickly.

This is our last morning, and the sound of the surf is irresistible. I peek my head out of our two-man tent and inhale the salty fragrance of the sea. The early-morning blue sky is a beautiful backdrop to the vast Pacific Ocean. Slowly I take a deep breath, refusing to let this moment escape any of my senses. Sitting at the edge of the ocean has to be my favorite place in the world.

Louie and I enjoy our last few hours relaxing on the beach and then begin to pack up. Our plan is to arrive at the oldest bar in Ensenada, Hussong's Cantina, with plenty of time to ensure we get to witness today's monumental event.

Built in 1892, the old-time western cantina never disappoints. The old, creaky wood floors and infamous bar, which is well known for creating the very first margarita, are part of the legendary ambiance.

Today we are lucky to find an empty table. A mariachi band of five or six men dressed in long-sleeved white shirts, black vests, and large, red, floppy bow ties moves about the room with their guitars and violins playing an old Mexican favorite, La Paloma. The energy in the cantina is contagious.

Speaking over the loud music and singing, Louie orders a Mexican beer, and I order one of the small but potent margaritas. Sipping our drinks, we wait. We are filled with anticipation and excitement.

About forty-five minutes later, an eerie hush falls upon the cantina. All of our eyes are on the TV hanging in the corner at the end of the long bar. For a moment the black-and-white TV turns white and fuzzy. I let out an "*Oh no!*" Thankfully the bad connection only lasts a few seconds.

I look around the entire room, and in this moment it feels like we are one big family, not strangers separated by ethnicity, color, language, or beliefs, but one big family with nothing dividing us.

Gathered together we sit in awe and wonder, watching the historic moment unfold. Neil Armstrong slowly climbs down the ladder from Apollo 11 and steps onto the dusty gray surface of the moon. All eyes are fixed on the surreal images when we hear him speak.

"That's one small step for man, one giant leap for mankind."

The entire room breaks into a boisterous applause. Bottles and glasses clink together, and loud cheering fills the cantina.

Today, July 20, 1969, along with approximately five hundred million people worldwide, we witnessed a monumental and wonderous historical event.

A good relaxed tired, we begin our trip home to Long Beach. Stress free, I gaze out the car window up into the boundless sky. With the glistening sun warming my face, I think to myself, *I can't wait for the sun to set so I can look up at the moon.* After today I will never again look at the moon in the same way.

* * *

Married life is proving to be not all bliss. Louie and I have some big hurdles and bumps to get through as we adjust. I feel a shift in myself, clenching down on issues that I fear could hinder our future happiness.

"Do you think you could quit smoking? You know it is really bad for you, and when we have kids, I don't want them around it." I become fixated on wanting Louie to quit smoking.

I'm also repelled by drugs and want to stay clear of those we know who partake. Our house has a steady flow of our single friends who are eager to have Louie join them for a night out and a few beers. I offer forced smiles and nod, reluctantly agreeing to Louie joining them.

In July of 1970, we learn we are expecting our first baby. I am beyond excited to be a mommy and start our own family. Even though a few foods make me a little queasy, I otherwise feel great and love being pregnant. Deep within me I've longed to have my own family and do my best to create a life different than the one I grew up in. I know it will be challenging, but I can't wait to shower my baby with love. We have our baby's room all set up and our hospital bag ready to go. Now we just wait for our sweet baby to arrive.

A little after dinner, a few of our friends drop by. Soon they begin to hint at Louie joining them for a few beers. Our baby is due any time, and I dread the thought of not getting a good night's sleep.

The baby has definitely dropped, bearing down on my bladder, resulting in several bathroom trips during the night. For the last month, I have not been sleeping well. I know when this baby comes, I'll need all the sleep I can get. Halfheartedly I smile and agree to Louie joining his buddies for a few beers. But there is one condition: he promises to be home by midnight.

The clock reads 11:45, and no Louie. I sit and wait and watch the clock. One o'clock, and still no Louie. I am so frustrated and angry, there is no way for me to sleep now. I sit and wait.

Finally at 2:40 a.m. I hear something and look out the window. Two houses down the street a car pulls up, and Louie gets out. Quietly he eases through our front door. I am beyond angry as my yelling echoes!

"How can you be so insensitive? I'm going to have a baby any minute, and you can't be on time so I can have a good night's sleep? What if this baby would have come while you were gone?"

In Louie's humorous style, he takes his forefinger and his thumb and puts them nearly together.

"Are you this mad? Or are you this mad?"

He goads me with his hand in my face. Then he puts his hands about a foot apart and continues, "Or are you this mad?"

I am exhausted, grumpy, and beyond his humor.

Two days later, on March 28, 1971, I wake Louie up in the early hours of the morning.

"I think this is it," I say while nudging him.

We scurry about, going down our checklist. I grab my prepacked hospital bag, and we head to Kaiser Hospital in Bellflower, only about twenty minutes from home.

Bracing myself for the horrendous next contraction, I can barely catch my breath, let alone talk. Scared and nauseous, I am focused on one thing: getting this baby out. Louie, sitting by the side of my hospital bed, holds my hand to comfort me while he chats with the nurse about fishing.

At 10:31 a.m., Travis Brendon Hockel enters our world. After four hours of intense labor, the moment we've been waiting for over the last nine months is finally here. A rush of activities ensues all around us. My body is shaking uncontrollably as I look around and watch.

All I want to hear is that my baby is healthy. There is a loud cry, and soon our dear sweet baby boy is placed next to me. I am a mommy! Holding my precious baby for the first time in my life, I feel like I am home! This is what I'm meant to be and do.

CHAPTER 24

Life and Challenges

Dorothy clicked her ruby-red shoes and said, "There's no place like home." Today I feel like a kindred soul to Dorothy. Home never felt so good. After three days in the hospital, our family of three is finally home. I'm so relieved Mom is with us helping out.

I wasn't expecting this roller-coaster ride of emotions. One minute I feel elated and beyond blessed; the next minute I'm on the edge of breaking down in a puddle of tears. I am mortified when I see the excess skin from my sagging stomach, and the maternity pants I said goodbye to are the only ones that fit. What's more, a looming, confusing emotion has hindered my desire to embrace nursing my son.

I know I have to make a decision, and I do. Because I declined to breastfeed, my upper torso is tightly wrapped with a breast binder to halt the engorgement that has already begun. The nurse at the hospital was indignant about my decision.

"You have enough milk to feed an orphanage of babies. You should really be breastfeeding your baby."

Her words heap shame upon me because I heard it all: "Breast milk gives your newborn the best start, the best nutrition." Now my breasts feel heavy, full, and throbbing like a pounding toothache, and I'm questioning whether I should have at least tried to nurse him. I already feel overwhelmed and loaded with questions about my new mommy role.

It has been a long day, and I can't wait to curl up in my own bed. With Mom and Louie taking care of Travis, I head off to bed for some much-needed rest. I'm bone tired and almost asleep when Louie comes in and sits on the edge of the bed.

"Your mom thinks we need to take Travis back to the hospital."

His words grab my attention, and I immediately sit up straight.

"What's wrong?"

Louie walks over and turns the bedroom light on.

"He doesn't seem to be breathing right."

I jump up and rush to the living room, where Mom is walking back and forth with Travis held in her arms.

I know instantly by Mom's eyes something is wrong.

"He hasn't slept at all. Not one minute. His breathing doesn't seem normal," she tells me.

Fear immediately strikes.

"Okay, okay, let's take him."

I quickly get dressed, and we are in the car and on our way within a few minutes. Once we arrive at Kaiser, they get us right in. A young doctor comes in, and Mom immediately starts the conversation: "Something is not right. He isn't sleeping and doesn't seem to be able to breathe right."

The doctor examines Travis and gives the nurse some instructions. She is gone only a minute or two and comes back and hands the doctor a sealed package. The doctor opens the package and pulls out a small tube. The two of them feed the tube down my precious little baby's nose.

"If he can breathe with this in his nose, he is fine. I don't see anything wrong with him."

In spite of the doctor's words, the breathing issues continue. I place Travis in his crib and tiptoe out of his room, praying he will sleep for a few hours. Mom needed to get back to work. She had been with us through the weekend, and having her near was a huge comfort. Now we are on our own.

As if the difficulty Travis has sleeping weren't enough, he projectile vomits the little bit of formula we can get down him. We are exhausted, concerned, and doubting ourselves. Many are giving the advice to just let him cry it out.

"You're spoiling him if you jump every time he cries."

Exhausted, I lie down on the sofa, hoping to close my eyes for an hour or so. After about an hour of sleep, he begins to cry and snort. This is the routine all day long and throughout the night for weeks.

* * *

Mom's voice echoes into my ear, "Happy birthday to you! Happy birthday to you! Happy birthday, dear Katy Sue. Happy birthday to you!"

It is June 18, my twenty-first birthday, and Mom's call is my first birthday greeting. I am a little surprised Louie didn't wish me a happy birthday before he left for work. I set my disappointment aside and begin putzing around the house.

At nearly three months old, Travis is beginning to babble and mimic our sounds and expressions. I'm relishing the significant changes, and I think he might even recognize me. The lengths between feedings have increased, and we found a soy-based formula he is able to tolerate. Thank goodness things are getting a little easier, or maybe I am just getting used to them. Travis is still only sleeping a couple of hours at a time.

Later that day, while Travis is down for a bit, I quickly hop in the shower and wash my hair. With the warm, soothing water running down me, I savor these few minutes of sacred alone time. *Maybe Mom and Dad Hockel will come over and sit with Travis so Louie and I can go celebrate my twenty-first and order my first legal drink,* I think to myself as I ponder what to wear. *It will be great to just get out of the house for a couple of hours.*

Forty-five minutes later, Louie walks in the door from work. I've been eagerly waiting for him, looking forward to having some fun celebrating. Right away I notice he seems distant, and I'm wondering why he hasn't wished me a happy birthday. *He must be tired,* I reason to myself. I pose the question.

"Do you want to do something for my birthday? Go get my first legal drink? Maybe your mom and dad could come over for a few hours and watch Travis."

"I'm tired. I'm going to go take a shower."

My heart feels unsettled by his response. Without looking at me, he walks right past me and into the bathroom. While he is showering, I sit alone as upsetting thoughts swirl in my head. I know sometimes he gets like this…pulls away for no apparent reason. But today on my birthday, my twenty-first birthday to boot, his behavior hurts and feels harsh.

Finally, out of the shower, he sits in a chair in our living room. No one is talking. He isn't even looking at me. We just sit in silence. I'm feeling frustrated but scared too. He is acting so strange and distant.

"What is wrong? What's going on?" I break the silence, inviting some communication.

Staring across the room, he finally opens up.

"I'm not happy. I'm going to move out."

His words land on me like a truckload of bricks. My heart begins to race as anger, fear, and confusion all begin to pulse through me.

"What do you mean? What about Travis? When are you planning to move out?" I prod, now physically shaking.

"I don't think I love you anymore. I'll take some clothes tonight and come back for the rest tomorrow." His words have zero cushion to them, and it begins to sink in that he is really serious.

Tears begin to roll down my face. Panic sets in, and I feel like I am going to vomit.

"Louie, why are you doing this? We have a baby. Please, please, don't do this. Don't do this tonight…it's my birthday."

My thoughts and words feel like they are in a blender. I begin to plead and beg him. Desperate, I fall to the ground in tears, imploring him to stay.

"Please, don't leave! Please!"

Not one of my words or emotional outbursts causes him to move toward me, to comfort me. Inside I know he is serious, and I am frantic. I continue to beg hysterically. My desperate pleas must have jabbed him, because he finally agrees to stay the night and leave the next day.

* * *

The sun is just coming up. My body is achy and hollow. I've had very little sleep.

I hear Louie rummaging through drawers in the dresser, pulling clothes out and packing them up. Once again I feel panic set in. I get up and go check on Travis. I pray he stays asleep. I don't know how I can take care of him and deal with the tidal wave of fear and anxiety I feel. *Please God, let him sleep so I can reason Louie out of this mess.* But no matter what I say, Louie's mind is made up. I pace through the house watching him load up the car and then drive away.

Now that I am at home alone with my baby, every insecurity held in my being is running rampant and consuming me. I am a mess. I can't eat or sleep. A few days pass, and I haven't heard one word from Louie. My sister Janice encourages me to pack up Travis and come visit them for a few days. Getting away gives me a tiny measure of relief, especially spending time with my sister and my adorable nephew, Greg, whom I love so much.

A week passes, and I get a phone call from Dad Hockel.

"Hi Kath. You know Nana is here, and she can't wait to meet her new great-grandson."

In the chaos I had totally forgotten Nana was coming from Pennsylvania to visit, and I had invited them all over for dinner! *Oh my gosh, how am I going to do this?* I ask myself.

"Kathy, if you could still have us for dinner, that would be great. Nana doesn't know Louie moved out, and we won't tell her. I will make sure he gets to the dinner." Of course I agree to prepare dinner.

With the help of my next-door neighbor, Vicki, who is like a mom to me, I plan a menu. Together she and I make home-made apple pies, and I find myself laughing again.

Adding her beautiful tablecloths over a couple of cardboard tables, we create a beautiful setting. With a big smile on her face and her arms full, Vicki carries over her cherished mother's wineglasses for me to use. Gently she places a delicate glass by each place setting. She cuts beautiful roses from her yard and creates a lovely floral centerpiece for my table. Wrapping me up in a big hug, she kisses me on the cheek.

"You are going to be fine, and your dinner is going to be scrumptious!" With love in her eyes, she exits out the back kitchen door.

Louie has been gone two weeks. I heard through the grapevine he was staying with his good friend Brian. The emotional turmoil that is rising within me is unsettling. I was just beginning to go a full day without being a complete mess. Now again my stomach is in knots thinking about seeing him this afternoon.

There is a gentle knock on the front door, and Dad and Mom Hockel arrive with Nana right on time. I lean toward Nana, and we exchange a big hug. Eagerness is decorating her sweet, round face. At last she sets her eyes on her great-grandson.

We get Nana settled in the rocking chair so she can enjoy holding Travis. Her eyes are fixed on her great-grandson as she gently rocks him and kisses his forehead. The beautiful picture before me momentarily sidetracks all my worries, and for several minutes all seems right and good again.

It isn't long before Louie walks through the front door. The energy is awkward and uncomfortable between us as we try to act like everything is normal. Still, even though pretending, I sense he is glad to see me just as much as I'm glad to see him.

It is past eight o'clock. Nana helps me get Travis ready for bed, and together we go lay him down in his crib. She places a kiss on her fingers and brushes them across our sleeping baby's forehead. It has been a wonderful visit.

I'm emotionally exhausted, but it has been wonderful to feel like a family again…even if Louie and I were pretending. I gather up the dishes and carry them to the sink. Dad Hockel moves close to me with a big hug. "Thank you, Kath," he whispers in my ear. Thank yous and goodbyes are shared, including Louie, who steps toward me and gives me a big hug.

"I'll come over tomorrow. We need to talk." A few words offer my breaking heart a little hope. The next day arrives, and Louie steps through the front door. Fortunately Travis is down for a few hours so we can have some alone time to talk. He comes and sits next to me on the sofa, which I determine to be a good sign. I turn and look at him and wait. I want to know what he is thinking and feeling before I say anything.

"I want to come home. I miss you."

The tumultuous swirling in my stomach that has threatened to take me down for the past couple of weeks can't be calmed that easily. I have been pierced to the core. I feel angry, and I feel scared. I wonder to myself, *What does this mean for our future? How can I ever forget this? Will he do this again?* I remember his words, "I don't think I love you anymore." Unable to still the nagging thoughts, I cautiously lean toward him and let him wrap his arms around me.

We spend all night, into the wee hours of the morning, intimately mending the damage. Or at least we try. It will never be easy to let go of the pain and fear I felt. Not long after Louie comes back home, we learn I am pregnant. In May our second baby will be joining our family.

May comes quickly. It is Wednesday evening, and Uncle Greg, Louie's brother, stops by to say hi and see his little nephew. Louie should be home in a few more hours. I always delight in watching Greg enjoy his nephew. Travis is all wiggles and smiles when Greg gently tosses him up in the air. Loud, happy squeals reveal Travis's delight. Then I reveal to Greg it might be time.

"Hey, are you up for getting me to the hospital?"

His face turns serious. "Are you kidding, Kath?" he asks.

"I don't think I'm kidding. Can you keep your eye on Travis while I take a quick shower?"

A little anxious, Greg responds, "Are you sure you want to take the time to take a shower?"

"Yes, I'm definitely sure."

While I'm showering, my contractions get stronger. I brace myself against the shower wall and take some slow, deep breaths when the bar of soap slips through my hand, hitting the shower floor and causing somewhat of a loud noise. Suddenly Greg barges into the bathroom with his back turned. "Are you okay?" he blurts out.

"I'm fine. I'll be out in a few minutes." We each laugh nervously.

I don't know who is more eager to get going, Greg or me. Soon Vicki, from next door, arrives to sit with Travis. I ask Greg if we can stop by his parents' house and tell them they are about to be grandparents again.

"Are you sure, Kath?" Greg is hesitant about waiting and delaying getting to the hospital, but I convince him we have time.

Mom and Dad are fully engrossed in watching an episode of *Benny Hill*. Greg and I sit down and intently wait for the sitcom to end, glancing at each other every now and then. Finally the show concludes, and I announce, "Well, we gotta go. We are off to go have a baby." Stunned and excited, they shower me with well-wishes, and at last Greg and I are en route to the hospital.

Greg had already called Louie at work to let him know. Once I am admitted, Louie shows up shortly after. My labor is intense but only half as long as Travis's. After being at the hospital for only two and a half hours, a beautiful baby girl is born at 12:31 a.m., on Thursday, May 11. Unlike her big brother, who was born nearly bald, her head is covered with an abundance of dark brown hair. It is a miracle. I was convinced the Hockels didn't make girls. I had prayed for a little girl, and my prayers were answered. I have my little boy and my little girl…Heather Marie. I am over the moon.

There must be an art to juggling two children, especially two children thirteen months apart. Whatever the knack is, I need to be a quick study. I think I am more tired than I have ever been in my life. Finding five minutes to myself to shower is a feat within itself. The saving grace is that being a mom has always been my dream, and I feel fulfilled. I just didn't know it would be this hard.

Travis has worn everyone out—my mom, Mom Hockel, my neighbor Vicki, and us. Today, heeding the advice of numerous friends, I decide to let him cry a little longer, hoping he will eventually fall asleep and sleep longer than his two-hour stint. Watching the clock I'm shocked he has been asleep well over three hours, which is extremely unusual. I tiptoe into his room to check on him. He is fast asleep, yet I see blood underneath him on the crib sheets. Scared, I call Mom Hockel.

"That's it. Enough is enough! We are taking him to a specialist," she says.

We learn that our sweet baby boy has severe allergies. His adenoids have swollen to the degree of nearly closing the air passages through his nose. Finally his difficulty sleeping makes sense. Unfortunately he is too young to be tested, so we follow the doctor's advice and remove the carpet and stuffed animals—anything in his room that holds dust. Following the doctor's suggestions seems to help him a little and helps me realize I'm not crazy or a bad mother…just exhausted.

* * *

Long Beach is having a heat spell with mild Santa Ana winds sending temperatures well into the eighties. Louie sets up a fan in the living room, which helps a tinge. The hot days and nights make sleeping difficult for everyone and add to my exhaustion.

I hear Heather begin to cry. Dog-tired, I drag myself out of bed and go make her a bottle. Holding her in one arm, I adjust the fan so it comes our way. Our sweet little girl is about six weeks old, and I am seriously wiped out. *Tending to two children so close in age would understandably wear anyone out*, I reason, and I keep pushing myself to try to get everything done.

It is Sunday morning, and thank goodness Louie has the day off.

"Could you please take care of the kids this morning so I can sleep just a little longer? Please," I ask him.

Around eight o'clock he nudges me.

"Hey, I think you need a break. If I can get Vicki to watch the kids, do you want to drive to San Diego and look at model homes?"

I lie in bed and mull over the idea. Even though I'm exhausted, a full day with no kids sounds too good to turn down and a perfect respite. Louie makes all the arrangements, and Vicki is all in. We are off to San Diego.

Long Beach to San Diego is about a two-and-a-half-hour drive. For most of the drive, I close my eyes, grateful for the solitude. Soon we find a new housing development and park. Both of us enjoy looking at new homes and capturing ideas for our house. Slowly we walk through two of the six model homes, taking in all the unique interior design elements. Once outside the second model home, I completely run out of steam. I can't take another step…not one. I stop and plant myself down in the middle of the cement walkway.

Louie looks at me, "What's going on? What are you doing?"

"I can't take another step. I'm too tired. I need to go home."

On the way home, I collapse in the backseat for the entire drive back to Long Beach. Finally, home, Louie pulls into our driveway, and I get out of the car and head immediately to our bedroom. Done in, I climb into bed and fall asleep.

"Hey, I'm going to McDonald's to get something to eat. Do you want me to bring you back something?"

I softly respond, "No."

A few hours later, I feel Louie sit on the edge of our bed. "I think we need to go over to Vicki's and get the kids," he says, nudging me.

"I can't. I just can't," I tell him.

Louie places his hand on my head. I'm burning up. He decides to call Kaiser and is instructed to take my temperature. It is 105.2 degrees.

"Please bring her in immediately."

The hospital is nearly full, so I'm given a bed in the ER. My temperature is now almost 106 degrees. Even raising my hand takes more energy than I can muster. I am half in and out of a fever induced haze while the nurses and doctors move about me getting an IV started and taking my vitals.

A lady in a bed near me offers her opinion: "You have pneumonia. I can tell by the way you are breathing."

I look up and think I see my mom. My vision is blurry, but I'm pretty sure it is her. I recognize her voice speaking to someone.

"She is prone to get pneumonia. She had it as a baby and several times since."

There is an unusual calm that comes with being so sick. I'm too sick to worry or even think about my children. Lying listless, I'm too sick to care about much of anything.

It turns out the lady in the bed next to me is right. I have pneumonia. They admit me, and after several hours I'm moved to the third floor. My fever is persistent and unyielding. Even with the antibiotics they are pumping into me, my body isn't responding.

Upon the doctor's orders, the antibiotics are changed to a sulfonamide. I didn't think I could feel any worse, but the next day I am even sicker. Lifting my head is difficult, and my stomach is swirling. My mouth has a horrible metallic taste that is triggering nausea. Soon I can't hold it back any longer. With zero energy I begin to vomit and vomit.

"I know it is the medicine they are giving me. I can taste it," I plead with the nurse to tell the doctor.

It takes into the evening before the doctor comes into my room for his rounds. I have been vomiting all day. He agrees I am having an allergic reaction to the sulfa drug they are pumping into me.

My hospital stay lasts eighteen days. Eighteen days away from my babies. Mom, Mom Hockel, Vicki, and Louie all hold down the fort while I am sick. Now after almost three weeks, I am almost home.

We pull into the driveway, and I feel ambivalent. I am so excited to hold my babies, yet I know the energy it takes to care for them. I'm still pretty weak and worn out. I give myself a quick pep talk, *You've got this*, and soon Heather is in my arms, and Travis is tugging on my leg, wanting me to pick him up too. Everything in the world feels right again.

Sadly, months later everything in my world will soon be turned upside down.

* * *

Dancing on a Crack in a Hollow House

It is a sunny afternoon, and I walk in the front door after a stroll around the neighborhood with the kids. As soon as I get the kids settled, the phone rings. I pick it up and hear Mom's voice on the other end.

She had not been feeling well. In fact, extremely unusual for her, she had missed a couple of weeks of work trying to determine what was ailing her. She had woken up early one morning and felt her balance was off. Initially she wondered if she might have had a stroke. When she placed her bare feet on the floor, one foot could feel the cold vinyl flooring and the other foot felt numb. Over the last couple of weeks, she had been to numerous doctors, and the last test was a brutal spinal tap. We were all anxiously awaiting the results.

"Hi, Mom," I speak into the phone.

"Hi, Kathy." In just a mere two words, I can tell something is wrong.

"What did they learn, Mom?"

"Well, they have decided I have multiple sclerosis." Just like Mom, she doesn't beat around the bush.

"What is multiple sclerosis? What does it mean? What do they do to help you?" I quiz her because I have never heard the words multiple sclerosis until this very minute.

The conversation goes silent for a few long, lingering moments.

"Mom, can they make this better? Can they help you? Can they make this go away?"

I only remember bits of her next comments.

"No, Kathy. There is no cure for multiple sclerosis. It will continue to advance."

180

I'm pretty sure she attempts to shield me from the horrific details about how her future will unfold with this diagnosis, or maybe she doesn't even know. Still, the words that echo through my being are…"There is no cure for multiple sclerosis."

Just like when you buy a brand-new car and you think very few people own the one you've purchased, and shortly thereafter you see the same car you purchased everywhere…it is that way with Mom's diagnosis. All of a sudden, everyone I talk to has a friend or relative who has MS. The details and stories I'm told are frightening and unfathomable that this could be Mom's fate.

Only fifty years old, Mom is struck hard when the disease surfaces in her body. She has to quit her job and begins walking with a cane. Then shortly after, she needs a walker. Strangely temperatures affect her differently. Cold feels hot, and hot feels cold. She dresses in thermal sweatpants to help with these constant temperature sensations.

It is midweek, and I decide to pack the kids up and drive to Downey and visit Mom. Maybe seeing the kids will add a little cheer to her day. We settle into her small home, and I look around to see what I can do to help tidy things up. Don had hired a lady, Maddie, who comes in every day while he is at work to do some light housekeeping and be with Mom. She is a lovely lady, and I'm so glad Mom isn't alone.

Sitting at her kitchen table with Travis on my lap, I watch Mom standing at the kitchen sink, resting against her walker.

"Oh golly, golly, I've got to go to the bathroom!" she blurts out.

Turning her walker toward the short hallway where the door to the bathroom is, she begins to move slowly. I watch her drag her left leg behind her. When she gets it in the right position, she is able to move forward another step.

"Can I help, Mom?" I gently ask her.

"No, I'm okay."

I'm sitting only a few feet away, watching her struggle. *Should I get up and help her anyway? Should I let her manage on her own?* My heart is breaking, watching Mom struggle to take a simple step. I hate seeing her like this! Hasn't her life been hard enough? She makes it a few feet, but it isn't quick enough. Urine runs down her legs, soaking her thermal pants and puddling on the floor.

Reality slaps me in the face. I quickly set Travis down and rush to help her.

"I'm okay, I'm okay. I just need to be quicker," she says with insecurity and fear resonating from her eyes.

On my drive home, I feel like I have the weight of lead in my stomach. My mom is deteriorating right in front of me.

* * *

Even with Mom's horrible illness, time seems to fly by when I'm busy taking care of two little ones. It is hard to imagine, but today we are celebrating Travis's third birthday. He is our sweet little curious boy who always wears a smile. Does he ever love his Pop Pop and Grandma. Since they only live a few miles away from us, it has been easy to hand the kids off to them for an hour or two or three. Dad Hockel often stops by on his way home from work for a quick visit with the kids. Both Travis and Heather light up with joy every time they see him.

Today the whole family is coming over. I heard through the grapevine Uncle Steve's birthday gift is unique and noisy.

Of course it is! It seems there is always a competition to see who can produce the loudest, most irritating toy to antagonize their brother, Louie, and of course make Travis happy too.

Ronnie, Janice, and Greg have arrived as well as Mom and Don. Our small living room is full. This very well could be the last birthday we are all together.

Travis is captivated by the kid-size set of drums from Uncle Steve. Uncle Steve holds Travis on his lap and instructs him on how to bang away so even the neighbors can enjoy. Travis's attention moves to the next wrapped gift. He rips it open and then moves on to the next. New fun toys are spread all over the living room. It has been a perfect third birthday. But the happiness won't last for us all.

* * *

After Louie moves out a second time, the struggles in our marriage persist. Louie and I decide a geographic change might be the only solution and the last effort to save our marriage. Moving away from family and friends and being completely on our own, we will either sink or swim. Louie takes a job in Seattle, Washington, and soon we will be heading north to the beautiful Pacific Northwest. I am overwhelmed with ambivalent feelings. I have never been to the PNW, and I'm excited to seek out a new beginning to try to save our marriage, but it is also gut-wrenching to leave Mom.

Our family—Travis, now three, Heather, soon to be two, and our yellow lab—is off on a big adventure. When we arrive in Seattle, we will need to search for our new home. With the proceeds from our house in hand and a new VW Van, we pull into the Hockel driveway to say our goodbyes.

We exchange hugs, and Pop Pop and Grandma smooch and hug the kids. As we back out of their driveway, our van loaded to the brim, waving goodbye and throwing kisses, I recognize the sad look on Dad Hockel's face…it is the same sorrowful look he had the night we said goodbye to Louie before he shipped off to Vietnam.

CHAPTER 25

Wellspring of Hope

There is something sacred about this assembly room—something that elicits calm and peace. This morning a wellspring of beauty from the morning sun has breached the floor-to-ceiling stained-glass windows unfurling light through a magnificent kaleidoscope of colors. Soaking in this celestial bliss, I'm happy I arrived early. Bothell United Methodist Church is an easy walk from our brand-new home in Bothell, WA. Louie and I both agreed church might help us.

I peruse the Sunday bulletin and watch families file into the sanctuary. Amused and chuckling to myself, the peaceful calm is thwarted when I spot a dad attempting to corral his vivacious young children out of a freshly tilled flowerbed. I notice I'm not the only one quietly giggling as a tinge of soft snickering echoes throughout the room. Finally, with muddy hands and feet, the youngsters are redirected onto the walkway into church, dad following close behind, discreetly but firmly imploring better behavior.

Returning my thoughts to the bulletin, I see a small paragraph that introduces Jack Crawford, noting his credentials and announcing a class he will be teaching at Edmonds Community College: "I'm OK—You're OK." Curious, not knowing Jack or what the class is about, I decide to seek him out at the end of the church service.

Jack is very warm and approachable. Although he is nearly bald, the hair he does have is gray to whitish. He has a well-groomed gray beard and wears small, round, chic glasses. Even though our exchange is brief, my curiosity has been stirred. In describing the class, Jack mentions a few words that fly right over my head.

"Transactional analysis, three distinct modes within each one of us that we use to process information and respond to the stimuli around us. In class we will dig into these different modes, the child, the parent, and the adult, and learn how they are integrated into our current ways of relating." When he mentions child, parent, and relating, I am all in.

I buy my book, *I'm OK—You're OK*. My excitement is largely tempered by old bits and pieces of failure. It has been a long time since I've been in a classroom setting, and now I'm thinking I've made a hasty decision. In spite of these brewing fears, I show up for the first night of class.

Feeling very uneasy, I consider taking my usual route of finding the nearest exit.

"Hi, Kathy. I'm so glad you could make it."

Jack remembered my name! Immediately my spirit shifts, quieting the negatives looming in my head. This little kind gesture has a tremendous impact. I immediately go from feeling emotionally disjointed to feeling valued.

It doesn't take long before Tuesday becomes my favorite day of the week. The insight I'm gleaning is like pouring trickles of water into an empty basin. Parched and thirsty for any insight that will cast a hint of light into my life's disarray, I sit in class desperately jotting down notes. I am being introduced to a completely new language, a language that begins to create small fissures into my troubled history, stirring up questions and more questions. Every once in a while, something Jack teaches creates a number ten Richter-scale moment. I tuck the valuable pearl of knowledge away to later mull over and over.

On one occasion Jack mentions to the class that he has a private counseling service. During a break I muster up my courage and approach him.

"Jack, are you taking any new clients?"

"As a matter of fact, I have room for one couple," Jack responds.

Even with the geographic change, our marriage is near rock bottom. With two wonderful children and a beautiful new home, from outward appearances we have it all. The reality is the many splinters in our marriage are festering. We are in agreement to give counseling a try.

Jack has a small office built onto his garage. Louie and I meet with him once a week for months. We begin to delve into our marital problems, and Jack becomes acquainted with our histories. At one point he suggests group therapy, where we will join three other couples to share stories and learn from each other. Together we decide to give it a try.

In the group therapy setting, Louie always manages to bring his humor into the discussions regardless of how personal and serious the conversations are. The eight weeks of the group counseling come to a welcome end. I am eager to continue, but Louie has had enough and doesn't want to continue with counseling. Our differences and desires are becoming even more evident. I need and want security, the white picket fence, and Louie hates the nine-to-five job and thinks selling everything and traveling the world with our two kids would be utopia.

In one particular session, I let Jack know that my mom is coming to Washington to live with us. It has always been a possibility, but a phone call from my sister Janice let us know moving Mom to Washington is imminent. She is bedridden from the impact of MS and unable to care for herself. My sister Janice has been communicating with me about the state of Mom's environment, which isn't good. Don hired help during the day to care for Mom while he is at work. He is still drinking and still very abusive. On one occasion he pulled the phone out of the wall so Mom had no way of calling for help if she needed it. At night he often passes out drunk, leaving her alone in her hospital bed set up in their living room. She is terrified he will fall asleep smoking and start a fire, leaving her helpless. The final straw surfaces when Mom lets Janice know Don is engaging with the hired help in the back bedroom. Turning Mom during the night is necessary to avoid bed sores. Mom finally has enough when one of the hired ladies shows up stark naked to turn her.

The plan is set into motion. Ronnie and Janice hire a bodyguard and show up unexpectedly at Mom and Don's home in Downey. Once let in they scurry about quickly, gathering up some of Mom's belongings, and remove her from his abuse.

Exhausted, Mom arrives in Washington. After a few changes to our house, we are ready. We bring in a hospital bed for her and set it up in our spare bedroom. I do my best to make her room cozy and comfortable.

Mom has a catheter that needs irrigating twice a day, and she doesn't have control of her bowels. I need some quick education, so I ask a visiting nurse to come to the house. Her straightforward comments pierce me.

"Your mom has given up. Please get her out of bed and dressed every day." I sit silent, absorbing her input. "Start by having her sit for five or ten minutes, and add a few minutes each day."

The only clothing Mom has is nightgowns, and her catheter presents a problem. I start making long skirts with an easy slip-on-and-off elastic waist. When I get her dressed, the long skirts make handling the catheter easier. Friends from church donate a plethora of blouses and tops. I am not emotionally prepared for the nurse's next suggestion.

"Your mom needs professional physical therapy every day. You can't provide this for her here. You need to look into a nursing home where she will get the help she needs." Mom stays with Louie and me for a couple of months until I can find a room for her at the nearest nursing home.

I can never erase the memory of taking Mom and leaving her at the nursing home. Only her physical abilities are failing her—her mind is still very bright and alert. This certainly isn't the case for the majority of the folks residing at the nursing home. She never complains, but deep in my being I feel I have betrayed her. She moved to Washington to be under my care, and I have moved her into a world where old folks spend their last days.

With structured, consistent physical therapy, hard work, and the assistance of a walker, she regains her strength and is able to walk the circumference of the nursing home. It is beyond encouraging to see these amazing improvements. Her roommate, Marvel, also has MS, and they click beautifully. I live five minutes away and I'm able to visit Mom and Marvel daily and often twice a day. I know Mom has no idea that my marriage is falling apart and about the stresses I am under. Then again maybe she does. Moms have special antennae.

Janice and Greg visit Mom

Making the decision to divorce torments me. Because of my own history, the last thing I want to do is take my children's father away from them. I've lost count of how many times Louie and I split up and got back together. In the end, the problems in our marriage grew enough to irrevocably damage trust and respect. After nine years our marriage ends.

After our marriage ends, I continue my weekly counseling sessions with Jack. With Jack's wisdom, patience, and consistent care, we continue to do the hard work of confronting painful experiences. Trauma had claimed its space in my inner world, hampering my ability to form my own identity. Who am I? What am I passionate about? What are my boundaries? What are my triggers? I am determined and excited to continue unraveling the multiple threads in my story and how they have shaped me. This work is difficult and emotionally grueling.

Jack introduces me to the theory of Maslow's Hierarchy of Needs. Maslow's pyramid of needs begins to link pieces of a tattered puzzle together, shining a light on tangible specifics. For the first time, I'm taking a hard look at myself. I can see how my childhood traumas influenced and hindered my emotional growth.

Maslow contends, at the most basic level, physiological, it is essential humans have food, water, warmth, and rest. This is a simple concept and makes perfect sense to me.

In the second level in Maslow's theory, safety, he argues that humans need emotional and intellectual security. As I embrace this idea, a flood of tears surfaces, overriding the pain I had so successfully smothered. My emotional being shifts from an adult to a vulnerable little girl held under cold water time and time again and to a little girl who never felt safe.

The hierarchy continues to the third level—love and belonging, a sense of connection. I am terrified to explore this concept. The words themselves, love and belonging, churn deeply suppressed pain. I have been convinced I'm not lovable, and I've never felt I belonged or fit in anywhere. My body visibly shakes as I unconsciously guard my hidden torment.

Closely connected to the good girl I have learned to portray is immeasurable rage—rage that needs to be dragged to an emotional surface and dissected without any anesthesia. Rage manifests in self-contempt and other-centered contempt: Why didn't I say no to Don? Am I to blame? What about the dashes of pleasure my body felt? Why did my mom not protect me?

During our counseling sessions, a profoundly painful question that has plagued me as far back as I can remember rises to the surface. I'm not even sure I have the courage to share what I've hidden for so many years with this man who has shown me he truly cares.

"Jack," I start…then I stop, unable to get the words out. Finally I force the words out of my mouth: "I don't know who my father is." His kind eyes lock onto mine from over the top of his glasses.

"Please, Kathy, tell me more."

It is a session I will never forget. He is now the only other person in the world who knows the secret I have carried alone for years. I share what my grandmother had told me repeatedly as a child: "Harold is not your father." I tell him how my mom refused to see me for the first ten days of my life. I tell him all I know, all the stories I had heard.

"If Harold isn't my father, could it mean Don is my father?" The floodgates of despair and horror break loose. I verbalize the horrendous thoughts that I have held hidden inside. A reservoir of fear transforms into tears and comes flooding out of me. Could this monster of a man be my father?

Jack and I spend several sessions delving into the secret I've carried. Then he gives me a homework assignment. I am to go to the nursing home and ask my mother who my father is.

We rehearse my visit with her over and over. We discuss how I could approach her gently because the last thing I want to do is bring her any pain in her weakened condition. The day comes, and I am determined to follow through with the assignment. I am determined to ask her.

It is after the nursing home dinner hour. Both Marvel and Mom are watching Lawrence Welk on the tube. I pull a chair up next to Mom's wheelchair. With only a few feet between us, I notice her glasses need cleaning.

"Can I clean your glasses, Mom?" I ask her and go over to the sink and wash and dry them. Handing her glasses back to her, I sit down next to her and begin to talk.

"Mom, you know I've been in counseling, and one of the things I've been working on is…"—struggling, I pause—"… something that has bothered me for years. I'm wondering—I'm hoping you can help me. I mean I hope you can help me. Mom, when I was little and we would go visit Aunt Mill and Uncle Ozzie, Grandma Kluck would tell me Harold wasn't my father."

With trepidation I force the words out: "Mom, who is my father?"

For several moments her big brown eyes carry a weight of sadness as she looks directly into my eyes. Mom's eyes never lie. Sitting with her I can see in her eyes the weight of sorrow she is holding. Then she drops her head. I wait. I wait, giving her time and space, but she just sits in her wheelchair with her head bowed. A lot of questions swirl in my mind…*Mom, are you okay? Can you tell me, Mom? Please?* Mom sits there, looking down, and never gives me an answer—and I don't press her for one. I place my hand over her hand, and we just sit in silence. Remarkably, even with the sadness I feel, peace washes over me.

Sitting side-by-side we are two broken and imperfect individuals who love each other, and that's what matters most.

I leave with the same question I had when I arrived, and I wonder if Mom even has the answer to give me.

I take some ChapStick from my purse and run it across my lips. Suddenly, out of nowhere, the thought of sitting in front of Jack creates panic. Am I going to be able to tell Jack the truth…that I still don't know? At this moment I wish I could take back telling him my secret. I want to hide and pretend it all away. Once again shame hammers me.

Sitting across from me, looking over the rim of his glasses, he interrupts the thoughts hounding me. Calmly, peacefully, Jack speaks, "I know who your father is. You have his eyes, and you have his heart." With a few words, he plants some beautiful healing seeds, and a tinge of relief stirs within me. But it will take time and hard work for me to fully understand and believe them.

Together Jack and I peel back layers and layers of painful memories. Inside the four walls of his office, I feel safe. With Jack near he guides me through delicate exercises. I imagine holding little Kathy close to my breast like I would my own child. I cry with her and for her. Jack gently coaches me,

"Tell her she is loved."

"Tell her she is not responsible for what was done to her."

"Tell her she is safe now."

I learn feelings aren't right or wrong; they just are.

Maslow's theory continues with esteem—respect, status, and recognition—and finally Maslow's highest level, self-actualization—achieving one's full potential. I have a long way to go, but I have taken my first steps toward healing.

While I'm entering dark places and learning new insights, Jack is instrumental in helping me replace deeply ingrained beliefs about myself. Jack talks to me about God's character and love. I begin to view my life through a lens of hope. I begin to embrace that I am lovable and worthy of happiness. Together we set little goals. I tape reaffirming notes to my mirror and refrigerator. Bit by bit, little seeds of hope are planted and watered, and new life slowly takes root.

* * *

Now on my own, finances are tough. I have to go to work, which means I need daycare for Travis and Heather. I seek out a Christian daycare because their care is one area in which I refuse to compromise. I rent a small two-bedroom house with an old oil heater that takes up much of the space in the tiny living room. I do my best to make the small rental home.

My hourly wage is $3.10. Although there isn't much money to go around, it soon becomes obvious I'm not good at managing the little money I have. At one point I am two months behind on my daycare bill. On top of being behind on my daycare bill, I've run out of the expensive oil needed to heat our small home. The kids and I huddle in front of the oven to gather some warmth as we get dressed. Because of the concern of a good friend, Vicki, Bothell United Methodist Church is made aware of my situation. They graciously bring my daycare bill up to current and pay for filling my oil tank. Love and care seem to follow me.

My visits with Jack are my lifeline to hope. Even so, it is a blessing I can't afford. Jack can tell something is off—he has gotten good at reading me.

"Jack, as much as I appreciate you and all the work we are doing, I just can't afford to keep coming," I reluctantly get the words out.

"Well then, we have a problem, don't we? I have a simple solution. You won't pay me for now, and in the future, when you can, you'll start paying me again."

I am stunned! My heart is overcome. I cannot ever remember feeling this kind of love. This man has become so much more than a counselor to me. The gift he is offering me expresses loud and clear my sessions with him aren't just about money—he really cares about me.

I can't imagine not seeing him or losing the help he is giving me. I also can't imagine not paying him.

"I can't not pay you, Jack. It just doesn't seem right or feel right." I barely get my words out, and he responds.

"Okay, I can understand that. I will charge you $1.00 for every visit. Now that we have that settled, we have work to do."

I continue to see Jack for several years. On my journey of healing, I attribute Jack's influence as having the biggest and most profound impact. Together we dive into the deep caverns of abuse and begin to unravel the damage done to my soul. With his wisdom, his gentle kind spirit, and his deeply rooted faith, he slowly helps me shore up the beginnings of a new and healthier foundation. I begin to see myself in a different way. I begin to see myself as someone created in God's image and not a mistake. I begin to believe in the person Jack sees in me. I begin to see the world through new eyes, and I begin to feel hopeful.

I've heard it said that people come into our lives for a reason, that it is not by accident or coincidence our paths cross.

Did God send me this special person at a moment in my life, knowing exactly when I needed him most? One thing I know for certain is that I would not be who I am today without his love and care.

Jack was many things to many different people. He was a husband and a father, he served in the United States Navy for twenty-one years, and he was a navy chaplain serving in WWII, Korea, and Vietnam. He was a passionate man, active in his church, sang in a men's gospel choir, enjoyed his Model A Ford, served on numerous boards in his community, and eventually became mayor of the city he called home.

Jack had a profound impact on my life. He was a lifeline on my journey to healing. Because I trusted him and felt his heartfelt care, I found a safe place to face my demons. I truly believe Jack was God's vessel pouring out a wellspring of hope that I desperately needed—a wellspring of hope that forever changed the direction of my life.

Jack Crawford
1928–2008

CHAPTER 26

God Whispers

Bill and I finish cleaning up the kitchen after dinner while Travis and Heather are distracted in their own worlds. Travis is creating one of his LEGO masterpieces, already an impressive two-foot-tall structure. Like usual, Heather is immersed in one of her favorite books.

The day is finally winding down. I make my way to the living room sofa and curl up with a soft blanket while enjoying the warmth from a glinting fire. I value the spare moments of solitude when I can reflect. Although we've only been married and in this house for seven months, it already feels like home. I reminisce about the significant changes in my life, how much I've grown, and how different my marriage to Bill is. I'm no longer living in a confused fog, and I'm more mindful of myself, my actions, what I need, and what I'm feeling. I'm creating my own safe passage through the world that was once a fearful and chaotic place. My heart overflows with gratitude for Jack and his gentle mentoring that helped me navigate the path to this inner happiness and fulfillment.

As I am absorbed in my blessings, an unexpected pestering thought overrides my peace and quiet. My thoughts shift.

Mom's fifty-ninth birthday is coming up, and I don't have a clue what to get her.

I want so much to bring light into her world. What is just one thing that would bring her joy? Living in the nursing home, her body frail from the dreadful effects of MS, she has very few needs or even wants, making this task of finding the perfect birthday gift difficult.

She doesn't need clothes.

She doesn't need knickknacks.

She doesn't need money.

What would make her smile, and I mean smile big? What would bring her that kind of joy?

"Family!" the internal voice softly whispers.

Well, I suppose I could buy some beautiful fabric and make her a couple of new skirts. I know she would appreciate my efforts, but new skirts won't make her light up.

"Her family!" Another nudge.

I'm definitely going to get her a special birthday cake, maybe vanilla with fresh strawberries and a creamy frosting. Certainly she'll enjoy a yummy cake. But in my gut, I know a cake won't make her light up either.

"Her family! Her family!" the inner voice pokes me again.

I sit straight up. "*Her family!*" I say the words out loud.

That's it! Family! Seeing her loved ones!

Every now and then, I get it right. I listen. I listen to the soft, persistent voice within me—the gentle, ever-insistent, re-occurring voice prodding me over and over. I often call these tireless nudges, "God whispers." And this is one of those times.

Now how can I make it happen? I'm stirred up, and my thoughts start moving full steam ahead. With absolute certainty I know having her family come to visit will be the perfect birthday gift and send her heart over the moon. I'm so excited that I rush to find Bill and share my ideas.

I've learned when plans are orchestrated by God, things fall into place. Mom's mom, Grandma Dartt, in her eighties, wholeheartedly agrees to participate in the surprise. She is 100 percent on board. Coming from South Dakota, she will let me know her flight details.

Uncle Bud, Mom's younger brother, enthusiastically replies, "Yes!" He will make the trip from California. Now to reach my sisters, Christine and Janice.

Mom's special day has finally arrived. It's Wednesday, April 21, and I'm as giddy as a child on Christmas morning. Dinner reservations at Traylor's are set for four o'clock. Uncle Bud and Grandma Dartt have arrived and are camped out at the Olympic Lodge Hotel. Christine will be arriving anytime. Unfortunately Janice is unable to make it.

Bill and I arrive at Crestwood Manor at three o'clock, giving us time to get Mom all dolled up for her big birthday surprise. I help Mom put on a fresh white blouse to go with her black-and-white-checkered jacket and skirt. Working a tad bit of magic with a comb and hair spray, I am able to bring a little life into her thin, chestnut hair. A beautiful corsage made up of delicate white roses and red carnations is held carefully in a small decorative box. Pinning it onto her jacket, I'm hoping she feels beautiful, special, and loved. Finally I run water over her glasses and rub them sparkling clean with a soft towel. We are ready.

Mom looks so nice, and I can tell she is happy to be with us and out of the nursing home for a few hours. Even so, I have yet to see what I'm hoping for…the real sparkle in her eyes.

Traylor's, an American homestyle restaurant, is one of the most popular diners in Port Angeles. We arrive right at four o'clock. Just as we requested, they have our party set up in a small private room. Pushing Mom's wheelchair into the room, within seconds I hear her squeal loudly! I have not heard that kind of loud expression come out of her...ever! I'm not sure who caught her eye first, but Grandma Dartt won't be held back, pushing her way toward Mom. With uncontrollable tears flowing down Grandma's face, she bends over, wrapping her arms around her precious, frail daughter. Mumbling imperceptible words, the two of them are crying and hugging each other.

Standing slightly off to the side, Christine is in tears too. Mom must have gotten a glimpse of her. Letting out another loud squeal, she stretches out her arms, "Christine!" Weeping tears of joy, the three of them are huddled tightly together.

I can barely catch my breath. Watching Mom overcome by all the love and joy is an emotional overload in the best way possible. And she has yet to notice her brother.

Uncle Bud and Mom have always had a special bond. In the old days, they both loved good beer and fishing. On the short side and well built, he can come off as a tough guy, but inside he has a big, soft, teddy bear heart. Watching his sister's health deteriorate has pierced him to the core.

Patiently Uncle Bud joins the huddle of affection encompassing Mom. There's another loud squeal when she sees her adored little brother.

Finally, we get settled at our table. Situated in the center of the table is an exquisite lavender floral bouquet Bill ordered. Loosely gathered with a medley of lavender and white blooms, it is beautifully held inside a clear cylinder vase. I am awash with gratitude as I continue to take everything in. Everything is perfect! Laughter, tears, and reminiscing are flowing in abundance.

Between tears I see beautiful moments of joy and peace on Mom's face. Truly I have not seen her this happy in a very long time. Yet it is obvious Mom is on an emotional roller-coaster ride. Because the MS has impaired her memory, every time she sees my grandma, her brother, and my sister, it is like seeing them for the first time. Tears of joy start flowing again and again each time she looks at them. There is no doubt a glorious infusion of love has saturated the room and her heart.

Mom's surprise birthday dinner is only the beginning of the perfect gift. The next day everyone gathers at our house to continue the celebration. All the ingredients to make an old delicious German dish, Kashganatels, crowd the kitchen table…flour, Crisco, cottage cheese, and Mom's red-handled rolling pin.

As far back as I remember, this family dish has been a much-loved favorite meal. We didn't have Kashganatels very often, but when we did it was an all-day affair. The flour and lard mixture create a dough that is rolled out and cut into thin, rectangular pieces. A heaping tablespoon of cottage cheese is then placed on one end of the rectangle. Mom would dip her finger in a cup of water, wetting the edges of the rectangular piece of dough. Gently she would bend the dough in half, pressing the dampened edges firmly together, encasing the cottage cheese mixture.

Next the dough-like dumplings would be dropped into a pot of simmering water. After seven minutes they would be removed and placed in a strainer, allowing the excess water to drain off.

Uncle Bud loves eating the Kashganatels right after they are scooped out of the simmering water. Multitasking, he holds a dish in one hand and eats the hot Kashganatel, and with the other hand, he continues to load more dumplings into the pot of bubbling water.

Most of us prefer waiting. After seven minutes in the simmering pot, the dumpling is gently placed in a skillet containing hot Crisco. In a few minutes the Kashganatel turns a crispy golden brown. At the very end, flour, milk, and the crispy remnants are whisked together, making the most delicious milk gravy. Pour the milk gravy over the crispy Kashganatel, and voilà! A flurry of memories, a taste of bliss.

I look over at the kitchen table. Uncle Bud, already in flour up to his elbows, is busy rolling out the special dough. On the stove a pot of water is beginning to boil, and the familiar scrumptious aroma is starting to fill the house. Sitting at the table, tapping her finger, Grandma is closely watching her son's methods. After all, she is truly the queen of this special German dish.

"Grandma, what is the history of this dish?" I ask her.

"Well, it was a very inexpensive way to feed a family during the Depression. We had to be creative."

With her eyebrows raised, Grandma occasionally adds her firm touch to Uncle Bud's already sealed dumplings—just to be sure they are tightly sealed, I suppose.

With the fire burning low in the fireplace, Mom, Christine, and I sit cozied up in the family room chatting. Christine is sharing stories and catching up with Mom. We share some memories, laugh, and eagerly await our first bite of Kashganatel.

The minutes, hours, and days of celebration seem to fly by. The clock is ticking, but the celebration isn't over. It's Sunday, and Bill and I have anticipated this day for several months. Travis and Heather are getting baptized this morning. We had arranged the baptisms months before planning Mom's birthday surprise.

"Kathy, I was only sprinkled as a baby, and I've always wanted to be baptized—you know, dunked," Grandma shares.

I am surprised and excited. "Okay! I'll let them know at church we are adding a family member."

"Me too," Mom softly chimes in.

Did I hear her right? I wonder to myself.

"What? You too, Mom?"

Smiling, she answers, "Yes. I want to be baptized again."

Mom was diagnosed with MS when she was fifty, and the disease hit her hard and fast. She immediately needed to use a cane for assistance and was unable to continue waitressing. It was devastating to witness the sudden onslaught of changes. But I remember other significant changes in Mom and not just physical. She made the decision to quit drinking and smoking. Going to church became very important to her. She read her Bible every day along with several daily devotionals. The changes were profound.

This morning the church is full of the usual familiar, friendly faces. Many of these lovely, compassionate people have become emotionally invested in Mom's well-being. Every Sunday when we wheel Mom into church, she is greeted with warm hugs and encouraging words of kindness. Many have prayed for her healing. One dear friend, Lucy, visits Mom frequently at Crestwood Manor. She will pull up a chair alongside Mom's bed and softly sing hymns to her. I know this brings Mom tremendous comfort. Now I look around the room, and I know I'm surrounded by a loving extended family.

Today we've been instructed to sit up front so Grandma, Travis, and Heather are close to the baptismal. My heart is bursting with gratitude. My mind has obviously been drifting because praise and worship is over before I know it. The entire room is now quiet.

Pastor Art Morlin, a robust man with a gentle spirit, dressed in a dark-gray polo shirt and black slacks, is ready to assist with the baptisms. The folks gathered listen intently as he begins to share the story of Mom's special fifty-ninth birthday celebration and family members who have traveled from as far as South Dakota.

The poignancy of the baptisms has struck deeper than I had imagined. I hear sniffles as Kleenex and hankies dab tears throughout the congregation. Pastor shares with the church how Bada Dartt was sprinkled as a child, and, now in her eighties, she has decided to be immersed. He shares about Mom wanting to renew her baptism. Then Travis and Heather are quietly nudged to move up to the baptismal.

Squeezing Bill's hand tightly, we sit, taking in the sweet moments of Travis and Heather's baptisms. Rising from the water, they are each given a towel to drape around them as they are ushered off to the side.

Eager, Grandma has already made her way up to the baptismal. Carefully, she is assisted into the basin filled with water, joining Pastor Morlin.

"Bada, we have spent time together talking about the symbolism of being baptized and what you are doing today means. Even though you were baptized as a child, you would like to reaffirm your commitment. Are you ready?"

In her no-nonsense fashion, she boldly responds, "Yes, Pastor, I am."

"Because you've professed your faith in Jesus Christ, I now baptize you in the name of the Father, Son, and Holy Spirit."

With one hand pinching her nose, she is lowered into the water until completely submerged. Quickly she rises out of the water, her face glowing with an enormous smile. For a few moments, there is a sacred silence in the room. Then the entire church breaks into a contagious applause and cheers! A towel is wrapped around her as she steps away from the baptismal next to Travis and Heather.

Once again the room is near quiet with only the soft, muffled sounds of lingering sniffles. Most eyes are on Bill and Mom as he slowly pushes her wheelchair up to the front of the church. Moments later Bill is back sitting next to me. I reach for his hand. This is one of those times I need him near. Maybe I'm tired from all the birthday celebrations, but for whatever reason I feel like I'm near breaking down in a puddle of tears.

Rarely do I look at Mom from a distance. But now as she sits in front of me a few feet away, I am struck by her thin face. Swallowing around the tight lump in my throat, I reflect on the many times I have wheeled her up to this altar, pleading with God to heal her. Wondering if my emotions were a hindrance to my prayers, I asked others to please stand in my place, hoping God, in His infinite love and mercy, would heal her disease-ridden body.

Today in front of me, my mother is thin, fragile, wheel-chair constrained. Silently, like clicking through a View-Master, a lifetime of images unfurls…the hardworking woman in the white waitress uniform; the tenacious woman with a can of Coors beer in one hand and a screwdriver in the other, digging a hole for a tetherball pole; the woman sitting at the kitchen table counting nickels, dimes, and quarters to pay her bills; and the bone-tired woman sprawled out on the living room sofa fast asleep. Her big, brown eyes, which once held passion, warmth, or anger, are now subdued. Today she is a mere remnant of the self-sufficient mother I once knew.

Sitting, dwelling on the sadness of Mom's frail condition, I believe God touches me. All the heavy clouds of fear, doubt, and confusion dissipate. The picture in front of me changes.

Mom's body is weak and broken, yet she is a beautiful picture of a God who understands and loves broken things. If we were unbroken, if our physical bodies never failed us, if we never made a mistake, felt sorrow, guilt, or pain, we would have no need of a Heavenly Father.

Soothingly peace washes over me as I look at her. I know deep in my being she is in God's loving hands. I know He is the one who can and will weld each broken piece together and make her perfectly whole someday. My eyes well up with tears as this beautiful moment full of promise seeps through me.

Pastor Morlin gently pours water onto Mom's head. "Having authority given to me by Jesus Christ, I now baptize you in the name of the Father, and of the Son, and of the Holy Ghost. Amen."

On June 24, only two months after her wonderful birthday celebration, Mom passed on from this world. On that glorious weekend, celebrating her and showering her with love, not one of us could have ever known the end of her time with us would come so soon.

I am deeply and forever grateful I responded to the promptings of that persistent inner voice.

And maybe, just maybe, if I listen carefully, I will hear God whisper…

"Welcome home, precious daughter! Welcome home!"

And then…a jubilant, very loud "squeal."

CHAPTER 27

I Will Always Remember

The days and weeks after Mom's death are laden with sadness. My world has revolved around Mom, visiting her at least twice a day. With Travis and Heather at school, Bill busy at work, and Mom gone, my world has a tremendous void. I am alone with a lot of time to think and remember.

I remember many evenings after dinner, Travis, Heather, Bill, and I would make the quick, five-minute drive to Crestwood Manor with a bowl of popcorn and tuck Mom into bed for the night. I remember her face emanating peace as we all stood around her bed, talking and laughing. Blankets pulled up under her chin, with a contented smile, she slowly savored the popcorn one piece at a time until the bowl was empty. Each of us kissed her cheeks and said our goodnights. I remember thinking how wonderful it was to not see worry, stress, or fear on her face. I remember thinking having her family surround her must give her a sense of security and peace.

My first visit back to the nursing home is difficult knowing Mom is no longer there. Driving into the parking lot, my throat and chest tighten as I attempt to fight back the tears. *Maybe I should just pull over and let it all come out,* I think to myself, but I don't, for fear I will never make it to the front doors again.

As I approach the nursing home, I remember everything—our usual parking spot and the large flowerpots flanking the front entrance. With trepidation I walk through the large doors. Florence is sitting at her post in the wingback chair, her eyes hollow, staring off into nowhere. I breathe a sigh of relief and gently touch her hand.

"Good morning, Florence."

Her face, drawn and slight, lights up like a Christmas tree when she sees me. It seems she might actually have missed me. Little does she realize her joyous smile brings me immense comfort. I needed to see her familiar face, a face that had become like family to me. And at that moment, I feel a warm connection to my mom, whom on this side of Heaven, I will never get to see or touch again.

Everything changed when Mom died. Yet eerily, here, in the nursing home, it appears nothing has changed. It is exactly as I remember it—Florence still sitting here in this chair, the same distinct pungent smells of cafeteria food and old urine, the muffled voices of nursing aids moving about doing their jobs, wheelchairs lined up against walls, holding frail, mumbling old folks, and the occasional loud and desperate plea from a resident forgotten on a bed pan.

I remember the many faces of the residents I'd grown to care about. Many of them have no families and consequently no visitors. Many don't experience the simple act of touch on a daily basis unless it's from a nurse's aide, rushing in and out of their room.

Instantly I remember and respond as I always have, greeting those frail folks lined up against the wall in wheelchairs.

"Well, good morning, Miss Sarah. How are you today?"

"Mr. John, you are looking pretty dapper in your blue shirt."

I continue down the line of wheelchairs. Then, unexpectedly, a harsh punch to my gut seizes my breath: I see Mom's wheelchair, now occupied by another bent soul who can barely hold her head up. Unprepared for this visual, I realize I didn't think this through. I didn't anticipate running into Mom's wheelchair when we donated it to the nursing home.

Fixated on Mom's chair, wishing so much she was still sitting in it, I reflexively run my hand slowly up and down the arm. My fingers touch the remnants of old Scotch tape. I remember writing in big, bold numbers, "44," and taping it to the arm of this wheelchair so she could remember which room was hers. How many times did I grip the handles of this chair, navigating her around? How many times did we fold it up and pile it into the trunk of our car for the ride to church or home? This wheelchair became an appendage of Mom, the only appendage left of her.

Overwhelmed, I turn away and quickly exit through the large doors. The crisp, cold air slaps my face as tears roll down my cheeks, dripping from my chin. I find a little niche next to my car, and the floodgates of grief open.

"I love you, Mom. I miss you! I miss you so much!" I cry out loud.

Still, I cannot silence an internal prodding to go see those sweet old faces I've come to care about. So I do. I return and find visiting them not only becomes easier each time I go, but in a beautiful way, my time with the residents feeds my soul and eases my sorrow.

I remember all the joy bestowed upon me from many of these age-tired faces. I decide to start a small weekly Bible study. Five or six residents attend in their wheelchairs, gathering around a table in a small room. I read a short daily devotional from *The Daily Bread*. It is a very simple read, a short story rooted in God's love and scripture. When I'm done I try to encourage a little conversation. Some share a little, meandering through hazy memories about God, husbands, wives, families and words I can't always make any sense of.

Next I pray the Lord's prayer. I'm certain if there is a prayer they might remember, it would be the Lord's prayer, and a lot of them do remember. Beautiful timeworn faces, some eyes closed, some open, recite the words that have been imprinted into their hearts.

"Our Father who art in Heaven, hallowed be Thy Name. Thy Kingdom come, thy will be done, on earth as it is in Heaven."

Near the end of our time together, I pass out a shortbread cookie and napkin, the only cookie the nursing home approves—no nuts allowed, and so on. The joy this little, plain treat ignites is painted over their faces as they intently and slowly savor every bite while verbalizing "oohs and aahs." Our thirty to forty minutes together comes to an end. Short, sweet, and very precious to me, our simple time together is bound in my heart to always remember.

One day I have a fleeting thought…possibly even one of God's whispers. *Let's provide them a special occasion, something to look forward to, something fun!* The thought continues to grow stronger, and ideas begin to blossom. They are big ideas, and I am not sure how I can make it happen. I want to bring a little happiness to the elderly community I have come to love, and I believe if God is behind my idea, the plan will fall into place.

My vision starts out small and grows—a luncheon for the shut-ins, food, entertainment, and most of all love. This will be a huge undertaking with many details to figure out.

After talking to Pastor Morlin and receiving his whole-hearted approval, I put the plan in motion. I obtain a list of nursing home residents who are able and want to attend. I also visit the other nursing home in Port Angeles and receive a list from them. Numerous volunteers offer to shuttle residents to and from for the big outing. Many willing hands offer to prepare home-cooked food that will be easy for the elderly folks to eat. I make a sign-up sheet for anyone interested in providing entertainment. The response is incredible—more offers than we have time for. We have a couple of meetings with all the volunteers, and I am tickled about so many creative ideas, the numerous volunteers, and how easy it is all falling into place. We are all in agreement: our number-one goal is to make sure every guest has fun and feels loved.

The much-anticipated day arrives, and residents begin showing up at church. The parking lot has a steady line of vans ready to unload our special guests. Volunteers carefully help fragile elderly folks out of vehicles as stationed greeters welcome each and every one.

"Good morning! Good morning! How are you on this beautiful day?" The church begins to buzz with chatter.

Joanie, situated at the piano, spreads lovely music throughout the large hall. My heart is bursting with joy as I recognize familiar faces being ushered in. It is evident many have made a distinctive effort dressing for the special occasion, adorned with extra jewelry, hats, gloves, and bow ties.

Young adults help get our guests situated at long rectangular tables decorated beautifully with potted flower centerpieces. Finally the traffic of incoming guests slows down. It seems most of our invitees have arrived. Pastor Morlin shares a short blessing, and numerous volunteers begin serving food to our elderly friends.

Looking around and taking it all in, I hear laughter and witness our volunteers comingling with our guests. It is the most beautiful sight. I am beyond pleased at how smoothly everything is going. A mere idea blossomed, and now all the planning is unfolding in front of me.

The volunteers are bustling around the tables, pouring fresh water into glasses, and helping guests unfold napkins. Soon the entertainment begins. A couple of vocalists sing a lovely arrangement of sweet old hymns, a violinist delights us with a beautiful rendition of "Amazing Grace," and a married couple performs a fun vaudeville dance routine. Our music director leads the entire room in a sing-along of old songs: "Oh, What a Beautiful Morning," "How Much Is That Doggy in the Window?" and "Que Sera Sera." The enchanting moment is inescapable. Remembering the old favorites, a harmony of sweet angels fills the room. High-pitched songbirds, mingled with low-creaking hinges, rise to the occasion, gently swaying with sweet smiles painted across their timeworn faces—a symphony of joy. *Thank you, God! Thank you for prompting this idea!* This is all I can think of as I soak in the bliss surrounding me.

Soon our special time comes to an end. Each guest is handed one of the small potted plants to take back with them. As the guests carefully cradle their precious plants, a line of wheelchairs awaits their return ride. A busy crew of shuttle drivers lines up in the church parking lot, making trip after trip until the last beautiful soul is delivered back to their home.

The successful event comes to a close with all volunteers on board helping dismantle tables and chairs, clean floors, and pack up leftover food. Everyone is exhausted, but our spiritual tanks are full, and our mission is accomplished. Love and joy flowed plentifully, and every guest felt it. We all agree we must make the shut-in luncheon an annual event. It is a day we will all remember. I have only one regret...I wish Mom could have been with us.

God certainly blessed me with all the many hours I spent with Mom. I remember everything, things I can't and will never forget. Oh, the many hours I was given to reflect, to look at the woman who carried me in her womb, remembering our journey together, with all the ups and downs and healing.

I remember sitting next to Mom's bed, holding her hands as she peacefully slept. As I held her hands, I was able to reflect on how many tips her hands brought to our kitchen table to pay our bills and how her hands soothed me when I was sick. I remember her warm, big, brown eyes and all the love shining through them. I'm certain of one thing: I was blessed to care for her and serve her. Now she is gone, and remembering every memory of her will have to be enough.

CHAPTER 28

Redeeming Love

"Have fun," I call out. I get zero response…not even a head turn. I'm not sure they heard one word I said, because without a doubt they are both preoccupied with their fun, creative attire and the day's festivities ahead of them. All spiffy in their costumes and excited for the school Halloween parade, they run out the front door lickety-split. Travis is all made up in a superhero guise, and Heather is in a fancy princess costume.

Sitting at the kitchen table after the morning whirlwind, I feel a peace and calm, a welcome reprieve. My alone time is sacred and scarce. *I better make a grocery list,* I think to myself, tipping the very last drop of orange juice into my glass while munching on my usual, cinnamon raisin English muffin. Adding juice to my list, I also jot down coffee, napkins, and toothpaste. Abruptly the phone rings, cutting into the blissful quiet.

"He's dead! He's dead! Don is dead!" Christine's voice comes shrieking through the phone.

"What? Are you sure?" I ask, stunned, as my heart drops.

"Yes! I'm sure. I'm positive!" she responds.

The phone call catches me off guard. Our conversation is short, and my sister's absolute certainty stuns me. Placing the phone back in the cradle on the wall, I try to untangle my thoughts. I should have asked her, "When? How? Where? Who told you?"

I glance at the clock. It reads 9:30 a.m. Instinctively I want to mark this monumental moment. Stunned, staring across the kitchen, my body begins trembling. Two words echo through my mind. *He's dead...He's dead.*

My sister's words continue to penetrate my thoughts. My emotions are a jumbled mess. What is wrong with me? I should be happy. I should be ecstatic. He is gone. The news has unlocked the jail cell of fear that has held me captive. I can now exit that prison...I'm free. He can no longer hurt me, my family, or anyone else.

How many times did I wish this man would disappear? And now he actually has. Is his death not worth celebrating? It's all so strange and surreal. Slowly I recognize a tinge of relief. Don is no longer on this planet! I close my eyes and exhale a deep sigh...yes, I feel relief.

With one phone call, my life has changed forever. Or has it? Bit by bit emotional shards of broken pieces cut their way to the surface, and a flash of terror fires through my being.

Oh my God, will this never end?

A harsh truth ferments within me: his death cannot obliterate the horrendous damage done to me. The trauma I experienced is not a flash in my life; it is deeply intertwined into the tapestry of who I am. It is not something that will vanish because he is dead, but something that has left an indelible mark—something I have to learn how to unravel and integrate into the rest of my life.

It would be easy to fall down a dark rabbit hole and revisit all his evil deeds, letting panic and fear resurface and take over, but I refuse to do it. Trembling, I make a go at getting busy, attempting my usual tasks of tidying up. I walk from room to room, my thoughts swirling, wanting to dig in and do something to distract myself from the lingering darkness…but I don't do anything except wander through the house.

A hint of nausea stirs in my stomach, so I steady myself against a wall next to the window.

Through the glass the autumn morning sun rests against a cloudless blue sky but can't hold back the nippy, cold bite in the air. I pull my sweater tight around my chest to ease the morning chill and my shaking.

Many of the trees stand naked, having released their leaves with a medley of colors gathered on the ground. Their beautiful, barren branches undeniably signify change. In contrast the evergreens stand tall, in full greenery, promising color and shelter, even in dark winter days to come.

Autumn has always been my favorite time of year. I love the vivid foliage, comfy sweaters, warm drinks, and curling up around a fire. My heart and spirit have always been moved by the grace and beauty of this season…the ebb and flow of holding onto the things we treasure and letting go of other things in hope of something new and beautiful.

Deflecting my thoughts for a moment, I step outside to breathe in some fresh air and ward off the nausea swirling inside me.

Beyond a deciduous hydrangea bush, I notice a beautiful, single, pale pink rose clinging to the stem that has been its life support. Intrigued by the rose's resilience, I touch the fragile petals. *Are they about to let go and fall to the ground?* I wonder. I lean down to breathe in its fragrance. There is still a remnant of its sweet scent. Something is drawing me to this strong, beautiful rose, rebuffing nature's call to let go. Even my gentle tug on the petals does not hinder its commitment to hold on to the stem that has been its source of life.

Unexpectedly tears explode down my face, and grief reaches into every part of me. Unsteady, I lower myself onto the cold cement front porch, trying to understand the tsunami of emotions pouring out of me.

Still, through my tears I continue to focus on the resilient pink rose. I am amazed how much of its beauty perseveres. Even through dwindling sunlight, cooler temperatures, winds, and rain, it endures, remaining beautiful and strong. Yet I know when it finally surrenders and folds into the earth, loss will not last and will not be the final victory. Every relinquished particle will birth a new, wondrous, and magnificent beauty.

I understand holding on, not wanting to let go. From an early age, I learned to depend on what was right in front of me. Predictability was my road map, guiding me through the terror and panic in my world. Moving into the unknown was terrifying. I resisted change because I was fearful of losing the little control I had.

Let go! Let go! I feel myself pleading with the resilient, delicate, pink rose. *Please let go!* More tears surge out of me as nature's beautiful message unexpectedly connects with my pain and my heart.

Can I find the courage to let go? Is my mustard seed of faith enough? Can I surrender all I've held so close to protect me? Can I trust the author of nature's message?

Fixed on the pink rose, I know for certain God's handiwork is at play. Every spring we wait with great anticipation, yearning for beautiful signs of new life to slowly peek through the earth. And without fail it comes…new life springs forth in all its wondrous splendor after the winter's long silence.

In this broken world full of sorrow and pain, we have a creator who has inexplicably bonded His creations to himself. He beckons us to let go and surrender to an unknown so He can cleanse, heal, and redeem us in love. Nothing is wasted in God's hands…not our pain, sorrow, sin, or beauty.

I am exhausted, but the stinging cold from the cement porch brings me back. My core feels empty, hollow. Then in that empty space, a swell of peace settles into my being.

Let go, Kathy. Let go. Step forward in faith. Surrender the remnants, the shards of broken pieces, and watch what wondrous beauty God creates.

As if this message had been divinely planned, I cup my shaking hands together and offer them. A soft whisper leaves my lips. "I give it all to you; I give it all to you."

Redeeming Love

And all at once the heavy pain
Fell from my eyes like rusted rain.
Cleansing my heart so I could see,
God's promise of hope beseeching me.

A pink and perfect resilient rose,
Clinging to the only life it knows.
A whistling whisper from the wind,
Bent its beauty up, around, and back again.
Hampered not, the rose clings tight,
Fighting the wind's relentless might.
Rooted in splendor, God's holy design,
No storm or strife can destroy or define.

Within the wind God's voice is heard,
"Let go! Let go! New life assured.
Redeeming beauty I will create,
From broken pieces: sin, anger, hate."

"Surrender!" The voice in the wind blew strong.
Oh, how is it you know my soul does long?
For hope, for love and a father's arms,
Where I am safe, free from all harms.

I breathed it in, this love so new,
To cleanse, heal, forgive, long overdue.
Let go I must, of anger and hate
And forgive all wrongs, leaving Christ to take.

The weight is lifted, my heart unchained,
Arising hope now flourishing unrestrained.
Beauty from ashes, He draws me up,
Redeeming love, my God fills my cup.

As if on cue, a gentle breeze brushes against my face just as
a couple of petals fall from the beautiful pink rose. Filled with
awe I look at the little flower with tears streaming down my
face. Change is coming for both of us. With my sleeve I wipe
my tears. Exhausted but warmed with hope, I exhale a deep
sigh, believing this is not the end, but merely the beginning of
something beautiful.

———————

On Monday, October 29, 1982, Donald Le Roy Milbrandt
died at age fifty-four. It is not for me to say where his soul now
resides. I pray he met the same creator I know, full of forgive-
ness, love, and eternal peace.

———————

CHAPTER 29

Love Is the Seed of Hope

June 14, 2002

This morning when I woke up, I made a promise to myself. I promised to savor every minute, every second of this special day. I arrive at North Seattle Community College early; even so, the parking lot is already nearly full. Taking advantage of my early arrival, I sit alone in my car reflecting. I wonder... *Is there anyone in this entire world who could possibly know or understand all that this day means to me?* I begin to think about my long journey and what brought me to this moment. My thoughts are drawn to one week...one extraordinary week in my life that undeniably left a profound indelible mark.

Two years earlier...1999.

* * *

The silence in the car is unsettling. I rest my head against the back of my seat, glancing over at Donna. It is hard to believe that Donna and I have only known each other for a short time. Like soldiers in war, our deep wounds drew us together. As I look at her face, I feel a weight of responsibility. I am the one who encouraged her to take this journey with me. Donna has not had any counseling, and her beautiful olive face cannot conceal the sadness and suffering I see in her eyes. Looking at her I recall the fear I felt when I took my first steps toward healing. My years of counseling were a life raft for me, and I hope this week will provide a beginning for her. In the silence I think to myself, *Yes, I am glad I asked her to come.*

Interrupting my thoughts, the blaring horn of the Evergreen pulling up to the Seattle ferry dock is a welcome intrusion. Soon my car is waved onto the ferry, and we are on our way to Bainbridge Island to face a battle alongside eight other women—a sexual abuse recovery week.

From the map on the backside of a brochure provided to us, Donna guides me to the Buchanan Inn, the bed-and-breakfast resort we will be staying at for the next seven days.

The inn, bordered by five-foot-tall evergreens, stands on the corner in a beautiful, serene country setting. The gravel driveway churns under the tires as I pull into an open space and park.

The instant we step out of the car, we are greeted by a handsome springer spaniel uniquely prancing about on only three legs. Immediately I'm taken aback by his obvious disability, which apparently has had no impact on his joyous spirit. This twist of fate does not go unnoticed. Soon ten women from all over the country will arrive at this lovely place to examine our hidden wounds that continue to cripple our lives. Inspiring, this sweet dog has lost something as precious as a limb and continues on. I'm hopeful during this week we too can overcome the betrayals that maimed our souls.

I stoop down to acknowledge his friendly welcome, and he nuzzles his wet nose into the palm of my hand. Then just as quickly as he made his entrance to greet us, he springs off to welcome the next guest.

One by one the other eight ladies arrive. Each of us is given a room assignment and invited to unpack and settle in. I'm directed upstairs to my room. It is a large bedroom, beautifully decorated in soft yellows. A gorgeous, floral down comforter covering a queen-size bed is inviting; I also notice a small twin-size cot and air mattress placed in the corner of the room. The privacy of being tucked into a corner draws me, so I gather my belongings and place them on top of the cot. Warmth from the sun is coming through a large window draped with wispy white sheer curtains. I step over to the window and look out. It is an absolutely heavenly view! Beyond I see a peaceful park-like setting, filled with graceful trees, a lush rose garden, several quaint wood benches tucked into cozy nooks, and rose-covered arbors that garnish narrow dirt pathways. This tranquil scene whispers of God's powerful presence.

Soon we gather in the comfortable living room where Dr. Dan Allender and two of his colleagues join us. I have read a couple of Dr. Allender's books, and I am astonished by his insight and ability to hone in so precisely on the devastating impact of sexual abuse. Now I have the wonderful opportunity to absorb some of his wisdom in person.

Sitting around the cozy room, each woman's apprehension is visible on her face. Most of us are strangers, yet we each know one certain truth about each other. "I have been sexually abused" might as well replace our identity on our name tags.

I quietly explore each face, intrigued by the details while wondering what their story is. A small stocky Chinese woman, I guess to be in her mid-seventies, appears to be the oldest, and the youngest seems to be in her mid-twenties. Nonetheless, even with our obvious physical differences, we each have made the same courageous decision to wrestle with painful memories and pursue a healing path.

The agenda for the week is laid out to us. Our days will be full and intense. Breakfast is served at seven fifteen, followed by a two-hour group teaching from Dan. The ten of us are divided into two groups, A and B. We will have intimate therapy with our group of five for two hours each day and one hour of individual counseling with one of the support counselors. In addition it is suggested we spend an hour a day journaling and meditating and an hour doing some type of physical exercise.

Dan does not proceed with caution. He has only one week to penetrate calloused, thick walls erected for protection. In his teaching sessions, I frantically take notes with a hungry desperation to capture each word. Our small group sessions of five are intense and cut right to the heart. In this small group setting, we lay open our wounds, recalling and verbalizing the horrors of being violated.

The names of our abusers are different—father, pastor, stepfather, coach, neighborhood friend—but the damage is the same. Each one of us is familiar with the feelings of betrayal, shame, powerlessness, anger, and self-contempt. As stories unfold it seems that sexual abuse was most often accompanied by physical and emotional abuse. By unveiling the pain and wounds guarded and tucked away in each of our lives, we become linked together by a love far greater than ourselves. The faces belonging to strangers a few days earlier now belong to my sisters who are a part of my life forever.

After full, exhausting days, our evenings are often spent gathering in the living room in our pajamas, talking into the wee hours of the morning. Our bond of loyalty and affection for each other continues to be nourished as we share our insights and observations. It is here God uses perfect strangers to uproot and expose longings I had deeply buried.

Several of the ladies begin to share with me their perceptions because of what they have observed in me. I am overwhelmed how each one of them shares the same thoughts. They tell me how they see something in me, a passion and ability to connect with hurting people. I go to bed that night revisiting all of their words of encouragement.

Near the middle of the week, I have an extremely difficult day. The group therapy is brutal as I share about my stepfather and his visits to my bedroom and my visits to his. Having stripped down emotionally in front of my new sisters and Dan, I feel exposed, raw, and vulnerable. I don't have an ounce of energy left in me. Yet here I sit with Susan, my individual counselor. Oh, how I want to skip this session and retreat to the comfort of my small cot, maybe fall asleep and push the pain of the group therapy away. *Boy, coping methods are deeply ingrained!* I think to myself and reflect on how I slept so much of my youth away. I silently vow to stick with the session and resist the old pattern of escape.

The question from Susan seems simple enough. "Who is someone in your childhood who made you feel loved?" I sit and ponder her question. No one is coming to my mind. I don't want to make someone up…I want to be genuine. At last the name Gwen is highlighted in my thoughts.

"Gwen was my older sister, Janice's, friend," I share with Susan. "Whenever Gwen would come to visit, I would run out the front door to greet her. She would stoop down, and I would collapse into her arms, resting against her large, soft bosoms. The embrace probably didn't last that long, but I felt like

I was wrapped up in a warm, soft blanket, comfortable and loved." Susan smiles, gently nodding her head in agreement, and we sit silent for a few lingering moments. Then Susan breaks the silence.

"Kathy, what is one of your deepest desires?"

Oh, my gosh, another question! I sit and think. Once again my mind is blank—nothing is coming. *What is one of my deepest desires?* Could it be my mind is blank after the earlier difficult group session? I can't think of one desire. Susan asks the question again.

"Can you tell me one of your deepest desires?"

I feel awkward and uncomfortable. *Why can't I think of something to tell her?*

Susan prods me, explaining, that for abuse victims desire is often associated with great pain. For this reason it is common to suppress longings and desires to avoid the pain. The room is uncomfortably quiet as she sits waiting for my response.

Words are swirling through my mind. *What do I desire?*

All of a sudden, with the force of a tidal wave, tears stream down my face. Immense sadness, guilt, and shame rise to the surface. Wanting to hide, I cover my face with my hands. I know exactly what I'm feeling and what I long for, but I am terrified to verbalize my thoughts. *Will she laugh at me? Will she think it is an impossible idea to even consider? Am I smart enough? Is it too late? After all I'm almost fifty years old!*

The seeds planted by my precious new friends about how they see my abilities to connect with hurting people are now connected with the kind face of an extraordinary man from thirty-four years earlier, Mr. DuBois. I sit vividly remembering the compassion of Mr. DuBois and the blank check he placed in my hands. Susan's prodding and my tears wash to the surface a longing that can no longer be held back. Through tears I tell her, "Susan, my deepest desire is to cash in an almost forgotten check and return to school."

At the end of the week, it feels like we have been there only a few days, yet also like ten years. The tapestry of our lives is forever woven together by love, our pain, and the deep desire to rise above the damage done to our souls. During our week Donna made courageous strides, some of us have only begun to face our demons, while some of us have slain enormous dragons, but one thing is certain: we are all heading back into the battle that we will forever fight.

* * *

Suddenly, sitting alone in my car at North Seattle Community College, the piercing noise of a nearby car alarm jolts me back to the present. Startled I check the time on my watch. Oh geez—it's time to get moving. I gather up my belongings and slide out of my car. Dressed in my cap and gown, I join the line of professors, guests, and other speakers for tonight's thirty-second commencement ceremony. After two years, many hours of studying, and hard work, a plethora of emotions is percolating within every fiber of my being. It is really beginning to sink in.

Soon the Seattle Symphonic Band begins playing "Pomp and Circumstance," and our procession line slowly moves into the auditorium and onto a raised stage. I follow in line with the professors and guests as they find their seats. Then I notice a seat with my name on it. I sit down and look out over the graduating class of 2002 as they file in and take their places.

I'm in the midst of watching my dream unfold. The music sends goosebumps along my skin as my emotions rise and tears begin to well up. The symphonic band is now playing "America the Beautiful."

A hush falls over the room when Dr. Peter Ko steps up to the podium and gives a warm welcome. Next faculty emeriti are introduced along with distinguished alumni. Soon the time arrives. It is time for the student reflections. I gather myself and stand up. Bursting with pride I adjust my gold honor stole and step up to the podium with my speech in hand. Remembering the promise I made to myself, to savor every second, I take a deep breath and slowly look across the room full of professors, graduates, families, and friends. Peace and gratitude wash over me. I open my speech and begin to share.

"Tonight is an extraordinary moment in my life, and to have been invited to share a little of my story with you is a tremendous honor. Years ago at one of the lowest moments in my life, I received a gift. I did not know the value of that gift until I had the courage to believe in my own ability to accept it.

"Mr. DuBois, the vice principal of Millikan High School in Long Beach, California, had always been lenient with me when I missed school. I think he knew something was wrong in my life. And there was. This day I had been asked to report to his office after a thirty-day absence from school...my longest yet. As I sat silent in front of his desk, Mr. DuBois, his face full of concern, took a piece of paper and began to write in large bold letters: BLANK CHECK. As he handed me the piece of paper, he said, 'Kathy, I am giving you a blank check. You can use it at any time in your life to return to school. There will be no questions asked, and you will know when the time is right.'

I quietly said, 'Thank you.' I folded the piece of paper in half and tucked it into the pocket of my coat.

"That was the last time I would ever see Mr. DuBois. From fifteen on I spent the rest of my high school years retreating to a land of sleep where I could hide from the secrets that I carried.

"Ten years later, in 1976, at the age of twenty-five and a mother of two small children who are now grown and celebrating here with me tonight, I first enrolled at North Seattle Community College and obtained my GED. It was a beginning.

"Twenty-three years later, in 1999, I attended a sexual abuse recovery week with nine other courageous women. Together we battled our enemies, and, like soldiers in war, our lives were forever drawn together.

"Helen Keller once said, 'Character cannot be developed in ease and quiet. Only through experience of trial and suffering can the soul be strengthened, vision cleared, ambition inspired, and success achieved.'

"The powerful experience of that week changed my life and led me to a long-buried passion: my desire to return to school.

"At forty-nine I accepted the gift given long ago to that emotionally crippled fifteen-year-old girl. This time when I returned to North Seattle Community College, I cashed in the blank check Mr. DuBois had given to me thirty-four years earlier. With that check I have redeemed the years that the locusts had once eaten.

"I have learned that the human soul is resilient, and the welfare of each of us is bound up in the welfare of all. I have discovered within me a perpetual curiosity like that of a four-year-old who continually asks, 'Why? Why? Why?'

"My instructors here at North have nurtured this curiosity by encouraging me to question, encouraging me to think. To each of you, I am grateful. To all educators here tonight, I would like to say, don't ever underestimate the power you have to touch and forever change the lives of your students. Many of you have touched me deeply…drawing out of me all that was waiting to be awakened.

"It is my hope that in some small way I speak for every graduate here tonight. No matter what challenges you have faced and overcome, each of you represents the victories and possibilities of the human spirit. Yes, tonight is an extraordinary moment for all of us. It is a beginning. In the degrees and certificates we will receive, we will hold in our hands a new blank check.

"As we leave here tonight, we need only to believe in our ability to accept it, cash it, and then, like Mr. DuBois, recognize that the gift we hold is even more valuable when we offer it to someone else.

"Tonight I celebrate with you our accomplishments, and I remember. I remember the generosity of a kind man who believed in me when I could not believe in myself."

Filled with relief and joy, I return to my seat. Soon the presentation of degrees and certificates begins. One by one the candidates' names are read aloud, and proud recipients are handed their certificates.

Oh, what a glorious evening. Simultaneously I feel exhilarated and drained. I find Bill and my family, and they wrap me up in warm hugs, verbal affirmations, flowers, and happy tears, celebrating my achievements. I feel loved beyond measure.

Most profoundly, in this moment, a love surges within me for that wounded little girl who loved school, loved learning, and so desired to please her teachers. *You did it! You did it!* I silently praise her. Undisputedly this night and her victories will forever rank high among the extraordinary moments in her life.

I believe the greatest weapon we have against evil is love. No one can stand in the light of love and remain the same. The incredible power of love can nurture, heal, and transform into unimaginable peace and beauty. The sincere love of many people in my life, including Mr. DuBois, has been the persistent voice calling me to survive and grow in spite of the horrible circumstances of my youth.

Many years ago a blank check was given to a frightened and emotionally paralyzed fifteen-year-old girl. She tucked it away like a treasured keepsake into the pocket of her coat, unable to believe in the hope it offered. This priceless gift, though buried for many years, never lost its promise. One by one the sweet seeds of love planted along my journey took root and blossomed, defying evil.

I hold hope that my story will give many others the courage and strength to rise above the damage done to them by abuse and find their God-given purpose through and beyond their pain and suffering. What is more, I hold hope our pain and suffering need not be wasted, but rather used for a divine purpose…offering love, hope, and healing to another wounded soul.

May I always remember never to allow sorrow and pain to have the last word. There is never an irreversible situation with God. The powerful force of God's love truly is the seed of all hope!

A Note from the Author

Dear friend…if you have come to this page in my book, it is likely you have read through some of my disturbing and unsettling stories. Possibly you are someone who has experienced abuse, and my story has stirred up your own painful memories. I want you to know you are not alone. I strongly encourage you to seek help.

The National Sexual Abuse Hotline is a safe confidential service: **1-800-656-HOPE (4673).** Additionally, I would urge you to explore the local resources available to you.

Unraveling the damage caused by sexual, emotional, and physical abuse is complicated, and the help from a professional therapist who specializes in helping abuse victims is immeasurable. It certainly has been for me.

I won't sugarcoat it. The journey from pain to peace, hurt to healing is not a linear path. It is hard work with many bumps along the road. The good news is it is worth every single tear shed and rigorous step taken.

When you begin to shine light on the darkness, and evil is given notice it no longer has victory in your life, hope begins to take root, and the weight you've carried diminishes. Shame, powerlessness, isolation, fear, hopelessness will no longer have a stronghold.

God can and will make beauty from ashes.

You are worth it.

To appoint unto them that mourn in Zion,
to give unto them beauty for ashes, the oil
of joy for mourning, the garment of
praise for the spirit of heaviness; that they
might be called trees of righteousness,
the planting of the Lord,
that he might be glorified.

Isaiah 61:3

Acknowledgments

Writing a book about the story of my life has been harder than I thought and more rewarding than I could have ever imagined. At times when writing about difficult memories, I had to walk away and return to writing weeks later. The truth is God wouldn't let me quit. He kept nudging me to continue. I came to trust He had a bigger plan for my story. With the support and encouragement of many people, I forged on, and finally you hold the results of many cumulative hours.

I especially want to thank my dear friend Angie Ellis. I am full of gratitude that years ago our paths crossed. Thank you for seeing my strengths and encouraging me to reach far beyond what I thought possible. Because of you I have changed and grown for the better. Thank you for sharing your wisdom and for our endless phone conversations into the wee hours of the morning. As the song goes, "So much of me is made of what I have learned from you. You'll be with me like a handprint on my heart."

I want to thank Rhinehardt (Ray) Hohenzollern for always speaking truth to me and saying just the right thoughts to keep me writing. Our common thread of abuse has created a deep bond and a beautiful friendship for which I'm grateful.

Thank you to my special friend Vicki Jung. You were my first true friend when I moved to Washington. You taught me to push against my demons and supported me with unconditional love as I took my first steps toward healing. I am grateful for our many years of friendship.

To Penny Robichaux, your unwavering faith and belief in dreaming big have been an anchor for my ship when sailing into headwinds. You radiate God's love and grace. I hope someday I can sit next to you and have a good ol' girl chat about many, many things while I absorb the warmth of God's light within you.

A special thank you to my sisters, Janice and Christine. You've allowed (tolerated) me traveling back through some excruciating memories, offering me some pieces to my own frayed puzzle. I can only imagine what emotions were stirred within you while graciously supporting me. Writing this story through my lens has only deepened my love for you and expanded my empathy for what you endured. We danced together, we danced alone, but one thing is for certain: our dance together in Heaven's light will be glorious for all eternity.

To my beloved children, Travis and Heather. Thank you for seeing the beauty in me and forgiving my many failures. The divine gift of your two lives has been and will continue to be my reason to strive to be a better human being. Wonderfully, I have learned so much from both of you. Always remember I love you more than all the M&Ms in the entire universe.

The gratitude I feel for my husband, Rex, grows deeper with each passing year. Thank you for your unending support as I journeyed back through my childhood experiences to write this manuscript. Wrapped in your arms when old demons surface provides the warmth and safety I need, and your strength and consistency help me continue to grow. Your wisdom to know when to let me stand alone allows me to become more whole and stronger. Thank you for your endless care.

I am eternally grateful to Jack Crawford, Mr. Whalen, Mr. DuBois, and Dr. Dan Allender. Thankfully your paths of serving and helping others intersected mine. You disrupted me, rattled me, and boosted me out of my own manufactured rut of comfort and protection. Each of you changed my life. Thank you.

Finally, and most importantly, I am forever grateful for my Heavenly Father. When I awaken in the morning and a familiar all-consuming fear seeks to devour me…I pray, "Fear not, for I have redeemed you; I have called you by name, you are mine" (Isaiah 43:1).

As I repeat this scripture, the hold fear has on me evaporates. Unlike when I was a child, I rise and face the day with hope. I do not fight this battle alone, and I know without any doubt who my Father is. He has turned my mourning into dancing and filled me with joy.

Christine, Kathy, Janice 2008